To Tom and Roberta,
thank you for being such
good neighbors.
With all my Love,
Jutta

Jutta Berndt–
MY STORY

JUTTA BERNDT

ISBN 978-1-66784-498-5

I DEDICATE MY BOOK, *Jutta Berndt—My Story*, to my wonderful caring children who areMargarete (Harold-husband) Dohring; Dorothy (Eric-husband) Madsen; Richard (Carrie-wife)Berndt; and Michael Berndt and to my grandchildren Brittany, Eli, Isaiah, and Brandon Berndt;Sarah, Joshua, Matthew, and Luke Dohring; and to Emma and Paige Madsen.

I also dedicate my book to my many friends at Grace Lutheran Church and School in Pocatello, Idaho, and to my friends here at Valley of Peace Lutheran Church in Hailey, Idaho. I could mention specific couples who are always in my prayers but then some may feel I forgot about them. My problem is that they are all so special to me.

I want to mention Pastor Jonathan Dinger who encouraged me by saying his dad wrote his memoirs and how much he has appreciated that.

I have to make a decision on what names to use and what names to leave out. I have so many wonderful memories of my special friends, and I pray people will not be offended because I could not write about all my friends. The names I did use are people I'm quite sure would approve. Using fake names really did not make sense to me. I just am so richly blessed with so many people I call friends. Please do not be offended. I love you all.

Last but not least, I dedicate this book to my departed husband, Manfred Berndt, and the wonderful almost fifty years he blessed, loved, and cared for me and the family.

Most of all I dedicate this book to my loving, caring God and Jesus Christ who have guided my life.

FOREWORD

by Marty Meyer and Kelly Meyer

In Hebrews chapter eleven, we read a description of men and women who did extraordinary things through faith. We often refer to them as "heroes of the faith." However, upon closer examination, we find that most of these folks were pretty ordinary, dare I say flawed, people before (and even after) God found them. I like to think of them as "*ordinary heroes.*" Let's be honest, often our lives are more messy than brilliant, yet God chooses to use us, simple broken vessels, *through which* he pours out His perfect love to affect mankind.

Jutta Berndt's story is the telling of an ordinary hero. You will read about a little girl in impoverished war-torn Germany who was more concerned with meeting the needs of the sick and hurting than thinking of her own concerns. This heart of compassion led her to graduate with a nursing degree despite insurmountable adversities. In fact, throughout Jutta's story you will be amazed by how frequently Jesus has used her ordinary life to make extraordinary impact. Like me, you might even say she's an "ordinary hero."

Jutta's life is far more than a story to me. When I graduated from Concordia St. Paul, Minnesota, I was placed at Grace Lutheran Church in Pocatello, Idaho, as the Director of Christian Education and Jutta's husband, Manfred, became my mentor and friend. My wife, Kelly, and I found ourselves around Jutta's dinner table every Tuesday evening hearing first-hand many of the stories that are contained in this book. Manfred and Jutta became like a second Mom and Dad to me as we went elbow-to-elbow and often neck-deep in ministry together for nearly ten years. My life has been significantly impacted and blessed by these two heroes, Manfred and Jutta Berndt.

Over the years, Jutta became an important example to me, not by any sermons she preached, but by the life she faithfully lived. Dear Reader, there's an important message in her book that I don't want you to miss: In every difficult situation Jutta demonstrates what it looks like to *keep eyes fixed on Jesus*! In my own book, *Epic Faith*, I write about a major principle of faith being "maintaining our God-focus." Jutta demonstrates this concept beautifully through some of her life's most dark and difficult circumstances.

As you read *Jutta Berndt- My Story,* allow a conviction to settle over you that *YOUR* simple acts of obedience and steps of faith can likewise powerfully impact those around *YOU*. Use the ordinary gifts that God has given you to bless others and watch Him do His incredible work! You may recall from the Bible the Widow from Zarephath who gave the last of her oil and flour to make a meal for the prophet Elijah. Or you might remember an old woman that contributed her last copper coin for the work of the Lord. I'm sure you know what Jesus did when a young boy surrendered his fish and bread while Jesus was teaching before a massive audience. The element that all these accounts have in common was that an ordinary person became a "hero" by simply offering what they had to give. It was the Lord who multiplied the gift and did the extraordinary! Thank you, Jutta, for sharing your modern-day life's example of such a timeless heroic truth.

Dr. Marty Meyer is the founder of Youth With a Mission Idaho, Boise-Cascade. He served in pastoral ministry for ten years and has over twenty-five years of mission experience. Meyer is an ordained minister through Christian Life Fellowship in Ontario, Oregon. He earned a Bachelor's degree in Christian Education from Concordia University in Minnesota. Marty holds a Masters in Missions and Leadership, and a Doctorate of Ministry in Spiritual Development and Discipleship, through Primus University of Theology in Phoenix, Arizona.

Marty is an international speaker and the author of *Epic Faith*, *Thirty Days of Epic Faith*, and *Mission Accomplished*. He resides with his wife, Kelly, and adult children in the beautiful mountains of Idaho. Marty is passionate about his family, the Great Commission, the great outdoors, and inspiring faith in the lives of Christ's followers. For more information about Marty or his books and ministry, visit: https://epicfaith.net.

EDITOR'S NOTE

Much as the book written by Jutta's husband, *For Heaven's Sake*, published many years ago after his death, the decision was made to leave the text in a format that honors Jutta's voice so that you hears what she wants to say, but more importantly, the manner in which she says it.

This style will enable you, the reader, to understand that she is just an ordinary woman telling her story about thirsting after God, finding God, and then making it her life's purpose to serve God in humbleness, joy, and reverence. She loves His people, His creation if you will, in a way that is utterly extraordinary and changes lives forever.

Cathleen Neumann

PREFACE

These are my thoughts and concerns about writing this book. Last night, I tossed and turned, and I could not fall asleep. I was thinking, who am I that I should write a book about my life. I have always known I was just an average person who has lived a very good life .I consider myself as not good looking and been aware of my bad eye. Other children made fun of me because of it. I was very self-conscious because I did not like to draw attention to myself. To cover up my insecurity, I have strived to always work hard to feel worthwhile. I never wore make-up because I felt uncomfortable and never really knew or learned how to apply it. My father did not approve of it. He said, "It makes you look like a hooker."

On the other hand, I also don't remember so much of my life because I took things as they came---took them for granted. I never felt deserving of the praise I often received. Looking back at all the letters and cards I received on special occasions, like my sixtieth birthday and also my retirement party, and the many praises, I did not feel I deserved them. I thought people just said nice things because that is what you did at such times as weddings, anniversaries, and special birthdays.

As I look back on my life and the things that I have kept, I am overwhelmed, and it makes me sad I did not respond to the people and get to know them better. I never kept a diary. Oh, I started a few times, but after a while, it looked like a waste of time. One day was like the next. I did write some of my stories in a book my daughter gave me many years ago, called the "Bedside Journal," and kept it. In there are some of the stories that have been told and retold over the years. Every time when I traveled to Germany, a new memory was shared that I hardly remembered, but my siblings do.

Just by hearing some of my stories, people who knew me a little better say, "You should write a book of your life." My pat answer is, "I'm not a writer; I'm not good with words."Then, Cathy came to me after church one day and said she felt God was sending her a message to help me write my book. After praying about it and talking to my children, I agreed to go ahead. I was not aware that she "is not" writing the book, but it's actually my story, and she is typing and editing it for me. This is an overwhelming responsibility since I'm over eighty-five years old, and much of my life has just flown by. I'm just an ordinary lady living one day at a time.

My original thought was, okay, I'll do it, if at the end, people will see that if God can change my life and make it wonderful, maybe, He will use it to help others too. I want my life to bring glory to God. Without God and all the people He has put into my life, I don't know what would have happened to me. He is the one who opened doors for me. He has always protected me. Early in my life many of the songs we sang and the words in them were probably a start for leading me to knowing God, only I was not aware at the time.

So, I want to go back to the original concern of why should I write a book about my life. Other people who became a part of it are the ones who deserve the credit for my life. It scares me to be so vulnerable knowing I have made many mistakes in my life also, I'm not proud for the errors I have made, and if the book is only about the good things, it is not really about me.

I wanted to share a story that started me thinking about making mistakes. My daughter took her daughter to college. When she arrived she began with orientation as usual, and after just a couple of days, she realized that, maybe, her goal was set too high and the expectations of time and money were too much for her. My smart daughter shared with her daughter about her own mistake in life. She had a huge wedding planned with her husband-to-be, and when invitations were sent out and all the planning was done, she realized he was not the right man for her. She was afraid to share that concern and got married. On the honeymoon, she knew she'd made a big mistake but stayed together for several years. She assured Paige, her daughter, that it would be okay to still change majors if she wanted to because she wanted to show her that sometimes we need to be reminded that we should follow our hearts and not worry about what others think.

That story made me think that I would be biting into something too big for me by writing a book. I'm still not sure if it is God's will to move ahead. I need confirmation and support. I received this confirmation by the way my daughters and Michael, my son, shared that they thought it was great. Dorothy, who now goes by Dori, was so happy and said, "I've been wanting for you to write for years already." Richard, now Chard, is the one who said, "What you wrote so far would be a great foreword." I read it to him over the phone while he was working in New Mexico. That was the kind of push I needed and felt I was within "God's Will." I still was aware of how unprepared I felt with this challenge before me. God has given me such a wonderful, fulfilled career and life, so maybe, it is one way to share it with my family and the many friends He put in my life.

A Little Story on Aging

Some people think that they can hide their aging process with lifts and tucks here and there, but God has His own idea of aging. In one of our morning 10 and 10s sharing, we had a story about this. God saw a picture of Mother Teresa and instead of being scared, he said, "Now, that is a beautiful woman."

It showed me and made me realize what is really important. Yes, we always want to look our best, but what is really important is not what is outside as much as what is inside. I usually am drawn to people when they smile and look approachable. I think beauty is seen in their eyes when you greet people. Most of the time I hardly notice what people are wearing, but I see their demeanor, their faces, and body language. I can quickly tell if they need a listening ear or a hug. Knowing the wonderful truth that God never runs out of love, never tires of loving people, gives me so much peace and joy that I want to be more like him. Love comes from God and fills me. Reading about the qualities of a woman in proverbs and how he describes her, most of us might feel like failures because there is a lot to live up to. It is easy to know what is wise and easier yet to fail God's expectations. He still loves us, regardless. This gives me joy to know.

One time when my granddaughter was sitting on my lap, she said, "Oma, your skin is getting kind of old, but I'm glad you are not getting old on the inside." That was quite a few years ago, but I was thankful she knew already then, that what is inside of us is what counts.

With age comes some advantages also. At work even the doctors would listen to me. You earn a certain respect with grey hair on your head. That works for a while, but now that I'm really old, people take it for granted you don't know anything anymore, so I find I have to stand up for myself. "You're old, so you shouldn't be driving anymore." I know what I can still do and don't listen. They call me stubborn; I don't care. It's my life. As long as I feel safe doing it I will. Sure, I'm slowing down—walk a little slower—but that doesn't bother me. The only real thing that bothers me is hearing loss, and I have to keep asking people to repeat things. I know it is easier to just tune out everything, but I don't want to do that yet—maybe when I get really old!

ACKNOWLEDGMENTS

I want to thank Marty and his wife, Kelly, for reading and making some needed corrections that improved the text, and, of course, also for sending a foreword to the manuscript.

I want to thank Sue Jenkins, my dear friend of many years, for being a beta reader and doing the final editing.

I want to thank Lana Gribas for designing the book cover and for her encouragement. She is, and has been, the art teacher at Grace Lutheran Church for over twenty years.

A special thank-you to Cathy Neumann for encouraging me to keep on writing and then typing all my hand-written words and organizing them into this manuscript. This was not an easy job with my many random thoughts and recall from so many different areas of my life. I'm thankful for her patience with me. She is a special gift to me from God. She has many of her own concerns for health, especially in this time of the COVID pandemic.

INTRODUCTION

I was born in Germany during the Second World War to an atheist family with a white supremacist father who worked as a lawyer during Hitler's time and a mother who couldn't cope and became abusive to me. This book is my journey from those beginnings.

At first it was just about surviving in a world torn up by hatred and the hunting down and extermination of those who were different. I just wanted to keep going despite the forced move from the destruction of my home in Hamburg, Germany, to other places including areas of Russian occupation. As a child of seven, I was so scared to be separated from my family. Despite these horrific beginnings, I found kindness and compassion in the people who helped my family and me, and others like me, such as the American soldiers, the local farmers, and the people of New York who I came in contact with when I arrived and others throughout the world.

This book is about my journey of learning, then accepting, and finally, loving the supreme being, God and His son, Jesus, whose understanding of me was profound. Even as a young child, I had a burning desire to help others who needed help in whatever way I could.

Jutta Berndt—My Story is a story of growth in my abilities as a nurse to help heal the sick, and if not, to offer comfort, as well as to live with, work, and love other people of different nationalities, and to work with the people and youth of America in many capacities. Little did I know at the time, that I was fulfilling the purpose God had chosen for me. Blessings and personal miracles come with service to God. Because of that service, it has been a joyous privilege to know and love so many people in my life for which I am very grateful. I feel humbled, and many times astonished every day, because so many people have let me know so enthusiastically that they love me back.

It is my hope that this story inspires others to seek God and realize His love and compassion and to discover the true purpose He has for each and every one of us.

CONTENTS

EARLY CHILDHOOD

My Arrival

I, Jutta Margarete Ellen Struckmeyer, was born in the back of my Uncle Frank's liquor store in Hamburg, Germany, on June 13, 1936. My mother, Margarete Struckmeyer, had labored at home for forty-eight hours without success. They had babies at home in those days, but Ididn't seem to want out so my father, Harry, and mother, Margarete, decided to alleviate the pains and lessen the anxiety by availing themselves of a little help from the store's merchandise. My Uncle Frank, of course, had to partake as well. With a little help from my father, I was delivered a breech baby at a healthy twelve pounds. I was in trouble from the start because I had three older brothers and my father wanted another boy hoping that he would eventually have a soccer team of eleven. Of course, he took one look at me and decided a girl was just fine. My proud parents took me home, and within two weeks, I contracted whooping cough from my older brothers necessitating a trip to the hospital. Unfortunately, I infected other babies in the ward and many died; however, because of my high birth weight I survived. Years later, I remembered this and realized that God was faithful to me even then, even when I didn't know of him.

My Childhood Home in Hamburg and Funny Stories

Three brothers and I on the steps of our first home in Hamburg on Blumenau Strasse

My first home was the house on Blumenau Strasse. It was very big with three stories and had a staircase with a round copper railing that ran all the way down to the bottom. I remember this well because my brother slid down it once in a while, but I was not allowed; however, it was fun to fly paper airplanes down from the third floor.

My father loved to go on the river named Alster, which is the right tributary of the Elbe River, which runs through Northern Germany. During the short time before the bombings occurred in Germany during WWII, he would take my three brothers; Peter at three-and-a-half years of age, Harry at two and a half, and Karl-Heinz at one and a half, as well as me, his only girl, Jutta. I was only two months old when we began our outings on the river in a canoe.

Later in life, my mother related to me that the boys were fighting in the canoe and tipped the boat. I fell in the water from my perch in the front of the canoe. Father reached out and grabbed me straight out of the water. I was fine and was happy. But, apparently, this happened another time, so my mother sold the boat. This was the start of my loving the water.

When I was two, I was potty training on a porcelain pot. I was tired of sitting in one place, so I took the pot outside and pushed it along the sidewalk while sitting on it. I must have made quite an impression for my siblings to remind me of this years later.

I believe my oldest brother, Peter, drowned behind our house in a canal around this time. He was about five years old. I believe that this was the beginning of my mother's depression that deepened over the years.

When I was three, we had a maid. She would cook our linens, under-wear, and anything white in big pots on a coal stove using soap made from pig's ears which was a yellow color. You had to boil the clothes for a long time, usually overnight. One of our neighbor boys swung me around like boys do, and my leg hit one of the hot pots. It fell and the hot water scalded my legs causing them to blister. I never did that again—a painful memory.

When I was about three or four, I recall that we had a nanny and a cleaning woman. She would wax the floor in the parlor. It was so shiny and clean, so I got into that wax and put some in my ears to make them shiny and clean. I woke up that night and my head hurt. I got in bed with my father (my Vati in German), and he somehow found out I had waxed my ears. He must have cleaned them out because I got better. I would never wax my ears again.

When I was almost six, in April, when the school year started, I was ready to walk down the front steps of the house and was so excited that I fell down the steps and hit my chin and needed stitches. My mother stitched it up, and it healed perfectly.

I also remember that my brothers had received a tute that looks like a big pointed hat upside down with candy, pencils, and stuff you need for school, but because of the war, I don't remember if I ever got one of those. It was a German custom at the time.

My mother had my second youngest sister, Hella, in April of 1943 at home. After the birth, she began to hemorrhage and my father took her to the hospital. I was not quite seven at the time and was returning home after school because first grade was only half a day. I found my new sister, Hella, alone, with no clothing. I promptly put her in my doll carriage and wheeled her to the children's clothing store called "Hundred Mark" to get her something to wear. The Deutsche Mark was the currency of the time. When my mother told this story to my siblings, they said I was a mama before I was seven. That story was told over and over again throughout the years cementing in everyone's minds, including my own, that I was naturally born to take care of others.

WWII Bombings of Germany - 1943

My father wasn't with us at the time because he was in the Nazi Army. He had to join in 1941 and, as a result, lost his American citizenship because he was born in Harlem, New York.

4

It was particularly hard on us because of his absence and because the bombings were frequent. I was about seven at the time and remember that every time that the sirens went off, we went to the bomb shelter. My brother, Karl-Heinz, who was nearest to me in age, sometimes didn't go, instead, he would take shelter in the cellar. I remember those six long blocks from our house to the shelter. We all joined hands to keep together avoiding being separated in the crowd, and sometimes I fell and would skin up my legs from falling on the rubble of the destroyed houses and buildings of Hamburg. We would return later to our home. Our help left because of the war. I remember she was Polish.

One time we went back and it was destroyed. We lived in the cellar for a few days while my Mutti (mother) notified the Red Cross of our situation. The Red Cross gave us all big nametags with all our family's names on it and my name was bigger than the rest. They hung from a string around my neck. I hated that sign. It was too big and cumbersome, and I knew who I was, so why did I have to wear it.

We had to pack up what little we had (a few trinkets that we rescued from the rubble) and the clothes on our backs and get on the cattle trains heading toward the East and a town named Jeetze in what was to become East Germany because there was no place to stay in Hamburg.

Jeetze - 1943-1947

It was long trip with many stops. We stopped each night because they bombed at night. I didn't eat much because it was milk rice and the milk was sour; it smelled and tasted bad. I had to hold my nose to drink it. I was to learn later that it had taken three days to get to Jeetze. All I remember during that time was the terror of being separated from my family, but, somehow, we stayed together. I was especially fearful for Hella and Renate who didn't do well with the cold. I didn't know what would happen to us—that was the biggest fear of all.

The complete Struckmeyer family in Jeetz, East Germany Easter 1945

When we arrived at Jeetze, we had temporary lodgings in a farmer's smaller apartment which was an attachment to the main house where the farmer lived. I remember his last name was Schulz. His father and mother used to live in that apartment, but I think they were deceased or moved in with their children, but, either way, they let my mother and us live there. My mother was nursing my younger sister, Hella, at the time. It was quite nice at first. We had a dienst madchen (maid) to help my mother and me and my siblings, who numbered seven at this time. I recall the apartment was nice with a bedroom downstairs for my mother and my dad on his various visits from the army. We had an attic where all the kids slept on straw mattresses in front of a wood stove for heating. I used to heat a brick, wrap it in a towel, and place it at the foot of the mattress to get warm. We had no running water and the outhouses were by the barn. One dark night, I crept out to the toilet and stepped on a pitchfork. It went right through my foot. I washed it right away, and, by some miracle, it didn't get infected. I didn't know it then, but I know now God was already watching out for me.

When we first got there, there was a post office, bakery, and delicatessen. We had some food stamps from Hamburg but they ran out. The farmers had to give their livestock, eggs, and much of their crops to the German soldiers, so there wasn't much for us except turnips and potatoes, very little milk, butter, bread, and sugar.

It was a good time in that I could ride the farmer's horse. My brothers made soccer balls out of inner tubes from bicycle tires and constructed stilts from cans and string. One week in the fall, all children got out of school and made money collecting potato bugs because there were no pesticides to kill them, and they threatened the crops.

At this time, the only dark part was the German soldiers. My older brothers went to the one room school for all six grades. The German soldiers provided all school children with grenades to throw at the Russian soldiers if they saw them coming. None of my siblings ever used them. One day they were forced to watch German soldiers shoot people. They told my siblings that if they didn't behave, they would cut off their fingers or worse. I didn't understand at the time what was going on about the Jewish people when my siblings told me of this many years later when I finally learned the tragic truth. At seven years of age, I stayed home to help with the rest of the family because my mother was subject to bouts of depression and would stay in her room for long periods, so I took it upon myself to take care of Hella, the baby; Renate, who was two years younger than me; and Gert, who was three years younger.

I remember one day very early in the morning, I heard a scream from my mother's room and opened the door realizing that she was giving birth to my youngest sister, Hannelore (until that moment I never knew my mother was pregnant because I was always told that babies were brought by the stork). My mother had applied for a midwife, but none came, so I helped deliver her with instructions from my mother. She was born March 14, 1944. We settled into a routine of making clothes from old curtains. We bathed at certain times in a metal tub in lukewarm water. On Fridays, the boys bathed and on Saturdays the girls had their turn. We slept on straw mattresses in the attic. We picked, peeled, and cooked potatoes and turnips every day—that became our staple food. We also ate pigeons, rabbits, and sometimes made soups with chicken.

We had been in Jeetze for a few years; however, as time progressed, things took a turn for the worse. The food became scarcer because the supply lines dried up forcing the bakery and delicatessen to close. I remember the hunger, the growling belly that couldn't be filled, then Hannelore developed tuberculosis, but she was strong. I slept with her and nursed her back to health, and calmed her when she cried, so she wouldn't bleed. I never came down with it—neither did any of my brothers and sisters.

I suffered from head lice at the time. My sisters and brothers shaved their heads to get rid of it, but I wanted to keep my braids. Things got so bad that my Mutti soaked my head in kerosene and wrapped a towel around it. It was burning, but she wouldn't let me take it off until the next morning. I had blisters on my head and neck, but the lice remained alive. We counted many of those lively and plump lice running around on the towel and pillow case when we took it off.

Diphtheria was another problem and many kids got sick and died from that, but we were spared. Then, we developed hand, foot, and mouth disease. I remember the pain, the blisters, and the sores in my mouth. I couldn't swallow. I hurt so bad. All my siblings had it, too. We seemed to have it a long time.

I think the American soldiers came during that time. They set up their tents in the fields. There was a soldier named Bill who brought his friends, and they fed us fluids through an eyedropper until we could sip through straws and gave us the first chewing gum I ever had. Bill, a tailor by trade, raided attics and made coats from blankets because winter would come, and all we had were summer clothes. They brought my mother some yarn, so she knitted sweaters for us one Christmas. They were the kindest people, but one day we looked outside, and the tents were gone. They never came back. I was about eight or nine then.

My father came back a few times, and I remember a time when we colored Easter eggs with beets and teabags. I also remember a little park in the town center, and on top of one of the buildings, was a huge nest with two snow white storks with a younger one. I was so very impressed with their beauty. I went back years later to see them while visiting Germany once again, and to my amazement, the nest was still there. My sister Hella and I went back to Jeetze to visit on one of my visits not so many years ago. I was amazed the town had hardly changed at all. The only real change was that the roads were paved. We visited the Schulz's place first. It looked deserted, but we went in anyway, and they were in the yard.

One look at my sister and farmer Schulz said, "Struckmeyers." My sister looked a lot like my brother Gert, who had often sent packages to his friend and another family while it was still East Germany. He also visited once the country became one Germany again. Even when Hella and I visited, things still looked gray and uncared for. Most people traveled to work in Hamburg or Berlin and spent some weekends or holidays in Jeetze. It was great to see theSchulz's, but, otherwise, it made me feel very sad.

The Russians Are Coming, The Russians Are Coming!

I think the Russians came in 1946. They took everything from the farmers— all their eggs, milk, and produce, and threw us out of the farmhouse to take it for themselves. They took all the jewelry and watches from people. At that time, wind-up watches were the only ones people had. The Russians, some of them very young, did not know how to keep them going, so they threw them in ditches. My brothers rescued them and traded them for food.

I remember we were forced out of the home we were in and had to walk—I don't know how far—carrying what we could, to a huge warehouse or some kind of retreat center in Jeetze. It was just one large room. We managed to make the best of it. I remember there were several bunk beds on the long wall. My brothers had made friends with the farmers so that helped keep us in turnips and a few potatoes.

We watched the Russians forcing the farmers to build barricades at each end of the town of Jeetze. It became a kind of a joke around the town about the "five minute commander" because the Russian commander kept shouting to the farmers who were building the barricades that he wanted it done in five minutes, probably because it was the only German words he knew. It was a bad time because we were afraid to go outside. Young girls who had a braid cut off signified that they had been raped by a Russian, and there were many of them.

One day my mother yelled, "the gypsies are coming, get everyone inside and lock the door!" Gypsies were known for stealing anything they could get their hands on, so we ran inside quickly. It turned out not to be gypsies, but my Tante (Aunt) Herta and her six children. As she had nowhere else to go, she came to live with us. I recall how Tante Herta helped me learn how to cook meals with not only potatoes and turnips but with all kinds of herbs, grasses, and even nettles.

Life carried on, but I remember that two of my cousins died of tuberculosis. I was ten years old at that time and held the youngest in my arms while she stopped breathing. She was so frail and didn't have the strength to cough. I recall that I decided that I was going to become a nurse or doctor and help children get better when they got sick. Tante Herta wanted me to put coins on her eyes after she died. I didn't understand why, but it made me feel strange. A while later, Tante Herta left with her four surviving children. I didn't know where they went at that time.

Escaping from the Russians - January 1947

It was a bitter cold winter and Father was in the western part of Germany during the war, and he escaped from either Russia or Poland. He had made a plan to get our family out of Jeetze which later became the eastern part of

Germany. There was a border between East and West Germany occupied by the Russians. We had applied and tried to cross the border legally, but when we got there, the crossing was denied, and we had to return. That is why my Vati and Mutti made the illegal New Year's Eve crossing because the Russians had something of a New Year's Eve party. My mother made some wine and took it to them ahead of time, partying with them, and showing them a good time.

The farmers became involved by helping us pack up our belongings in hay wagons pulled by horses with a tarp overtop. We were under featherbeds to keep us warm. All eight children were taken by the farmers in the middle of the night to the border after leaving the Russian guards drunk and passed out. It was a joyous reunion between my father and us. He was on the other side of the border with a big truck. I remember that my brother Karl-Heinz, who was twelve years old at the time, had frostbitten ears because he wanted to sit up with the farmer who drove us to the border. The farmers helped us to get in the truck, and they returned to their farms safely. Then, we moved to Bergedorf, Germany, close to Hamburg, where my dad had rented an apartment for us.

Bergedorf–Suburb of Hamburg, Germany - 1947-1952

Second floor apartment in Bergedorf, Germany 1947

My father rented a second floor apartment that had been occupied by British soldiers earlier in the war. It seemed very large to me. The four boys were in one bedroom and the four girls, including me, were in the other. My parents had a nice bedroom, and a large den was situated next to it. Off the den was the hallway to the other rooms, the kitchen, and the bathroom with a bathtub. The bathroom had a gas heater, so we had nice warm baths.

The large kitchen had running water which was not heated and an old fashioned woodstove. There was a large table to eat on and do homework with the children. At the entrance of the apartment, there was a small room with a bed and small bathroom with a sink and toilet. There was also an upright piano. My brother Harry always practiced playing the piano. That small room became the infirmary if anyone of the family got a cold or sick, they were quarantined in there. We were served chamomile tea and

13

cookies and water until there was no more cough or fever. It was almost a treat to be sick. The dining room held a large table and benches.

I recall there was a small, freestanding, pot-bellied stove for heating and a little bit of coal to keep it working. It was cold when we arrived, so we stayed close to the stove to keep warm and used this room for gymnastics because everyone liked to keep active. My job, at the time, was to knit stockings and mittens for everyone. I think a brother of mine found some lice powder left from the British in the big fireplace in the den, and my father found some ammunition left from the soldiers in there, as well.

Vati had to go back to the war and Mutti slumped into depression again, staying in the living room, demanding coffee and cigarettes constantly. In order to keep her happy and not abusive, my brothers would collect cigarette butts on the streets. We could get the cigarette papers at the store, take out any tobacco from the discarded cigarettes, and roll her new ones. That became a full time job for them.

Many times I had to mix the regular coffee with what they called Ersatz Coffee because it was cheap, and we got a lot because we were on a budget. I think it had chicory in it, but I was afraid that if she knew, she would abuse me verbally or physically. It was the same thing if cigarettes ran out. One of the times when I had no more cigarettes or coffee, my mother pushed me out of the second story window where I was knitting and enjoying the sunshine on my back. I landed in gooseberry bushes and was quite a sight for a while, but I felt that it could have been a lot worse because each floor had twelve foot ceilings. I didn't get broken bones or die from hitting my head. I was very afraid of my mother at that time, and all of us did everything we could to keep her happy, but sometimes we couldn't. One time, one of my older brothers was hit in the head with one of my mother's high heeled shoes leaving a big hole in it because he was closest to her when she went into one of her rages.

The landlord complained about the gymnastics because he lived below us and could hear and see the results of our movements because it got his lights swinging and made him afraid that they would fall. When that happened, I was blamed for it no matter if it was me or not. I always felt my mother was jealous of my father's love for me so that made me a target when things went wrong during his intermittent absences. I think he was in jail for war crimes. I'm not sure. He escaped jail several times but was always recaptured.

It was a hard time for me because I took care of the family. I didn't go to school like the other children. My mother was unable to care for us and stayed in her room most of the time.

I remember my siblings and I going to the Red Cross once a month to get a dose of cod liver oil because they wanted to make sure that children in that area got something to help with malnourishment. Everyone had to take a tablespoon. I recall the horrible taste. At one time, the Red Cross wanted to put my siblings and me into homes because my mother couldn't care for us, but I talked them out of it. I explained that I would take care of them and told them my father was coming back very soon.

I became very busy finding ways to keep our family fed and together. I went on a train to Hamburg to get some money from my father's parents to help feed everyone. My mother was very upset about this because they were the same parents who earlier had disowned their son (my father) for marrying my mother because she was not from a prosperous family and was uneducated.

The allowance helped but didn't go far enough for eight children and my mother who wanted special food, so I had to get daily soup from the soup kitchen. I remember that Wednesday was fish soup—not like clam chowder—but with bones floating around in it. None of us liked it, but we were hungry, so we ate it. I worked hard doing our laundry by hand in the bathtub. Sunday was for soaking the clothes, Monday was for washing them up, Tuesday and Wednesday were for hanging and ironing because we only had two sets of clothes. When my brothers walked home from school, they would pick fruit off of other people's trees because people weren't picking the fruit, and we needed it. I remember using my best butter to get the tar to slide off of my brother's hair. He was underneath a newly tarred roof while picking, and it dropped on his head and stuck in his hair.

I earned extra money by taking care of four children who lived across the street from us .I did this for a widow who had lost her husband in the war. She related to me that he was killed on a motorcycle while serving in Hitler's army. She received money from the government but felt it wasn't enough, so she went to work to feed herself and her children. I took care of her two boys, ages four and eight, who were hemophiliacs. Their knees were huge, swollen, and ugly. They got hurt a lot. The girls, ages three and five, were beautiful. When we went anywhere, which wasn't very often, I would carry the four-year-old boy because he wasn't very careful and would bump himself and bleed.

I liked taking care of them because I was helping them, and that was when it was confirmed in my mind that I would be a nurse when I grew up. I took care of another neighbor in his forties who lived by himself. He had cancer of the tongue and throat. There was no treatment for him. I spoon fed him, and one day, his tongue came off onto the spoon. He bled and died a few days later. I cried and cried for him wondering why people had to suffer like that.

Things became much better when my father was released from prison. I remember how much fun it was when he came home. My father was a lawyer before he went into the army, so he resumed that work later in Hamburg. He took the train from Bergedorf into Hamburg every day. It was about a thirty-minute commute. We would always wait impatiently for him to come home. I did not know what he was doing in Hamburg at the time, but times were good when he was there. Mother was much better when he was home, so things settled into a routine.

Vati helped us with homework and taught us to play piano (he always found a way to get a grand piano). Father helped us with homework, but also taught us to play chess and all kinds of things. I knew he loved all of us very much by taking the time to do things with us when he was not working. Sundays, when it was nice, our family would go into the forest close to our apartment for long hikes picking blueberries and small mushrooms called pfifferlinge. We chased and teased each other all day enjoying the time spent with family. My older brother even owned a bicycle. Those were my best memories.

I recalled another story while we were living there. At the bottom of the hill of this big house which had been turned into single floor apartments (we lived on the second floor) was a river named Bille. My brothers had found an old wooden kayak in the basement of this house, and in the spring, they carried it down to the river and took turns going down it, then carrying it back up so another person could use it and do the same thing. I remember the water was cold, but I loved kayaking in it and swimming.

I recollect that I did a little roller skating using the kind of skates with metal wheels and clips to attach to your shoes. I also recall that behind our place was a sports stadium and some tennis courts. My siblings and I would watch soccer games and school sports in the spring and summer, and in the winter, we would sled and ski with old equipment we found in the basement. My brothers earned some German marks (German money at the time) fetching tennis balls for people who played tennis.

When my father was around the grand piano, we all joined him. All of us liked to sing and singing songs around the piano with him (many of them were about Christian themes even though my father was an atheist) was always a happy, memorable time. Quite a few songs were drinking songs, war songs, or classical music, or just about anything that someone wanted him to play. Neighbors' children would come to our apartment and would enjoy singing with us. All of us had good voices, so we enjoyed the singing. Many times when I rode the train to Hamburg to get money from my grandparents after my dad was gone, I would take a window seat and sing many of those songs. Many of the songs would sometimes bring a yearning in my heart for something, but I didn't know what it was. Later, while sleeping, I wondered about God and Jesus in those songs.

During the time my father was home, I could go to school. At that time, I was in sixth grade. I met Marianne at school. She was the only friend I had outside my family. Marianne had a mom and two sisters. They lived in a small row house apartment. Marianne loved coming to our apartment and enjoyed singing and playing with us. She also had her eye on my older brother.

I am the shortest sixth grade student in the front. Marianne is to the left
of me. This was the only year I was able to attend school 1950

Marianne was born into a Christian family. They went to church every Sunday, prayed at home, and at meals. I was uncomfortable with this at first because my father was an atheist and didn't believe in God or Jesus even though he was raised "a Catholic." He forbade us to talk about God but played spiritual music. I went to church with my friend a few times—never telling my parents. The pastor at that church asked me to join the Friday night confirmation class, and I did. I told my parents that I was going to gymnastics. I studied deep into the night the information needed to pass my confirmation class. The day I was to be confirmed, I debated whether to tell my parents, but I just couldn't. The confirmation dress for girls was maroon, so I made my own. I spent the weekend with Marianne, was baptized, and confirmed.

My parents, somehow, heard about it, so for my punishment, I had to do all the dishes from the weekend (dishes from two adults and seven children since I had been at Marianne's). I had to heat the water to do them all. It was quite overwhelming, but I smiled and sang songs to make it less of a chore. My parents were very upset, but felt at the age of fourteen, that I was old enough to make some choices.

I remember a funny story about my father. He had a partial set of teeth in his mouth, and at night he always put them in a cup of water in the bathroom. One day he got up and was a little upset. He couldn't find his teeth. He made us go through all the garbage of a full week which was monumental. We did it, and as we finished and there was no set of teeth, I looked at him and said, "Father, I think you have them in your mouth." There they were, plain as day. He apologized. He had forgotten to take them out the previous night. We put all the garbage back.

Vati had to go back to jail because of some shady business he had been caught doing with his brother-in-law. They stole a big church bell and sold it. This was what my sister told me later.

I was about fourteen and my mother got demanding and mean again because Father was gone. I remember climbing onto the shelf in the closet, (not a built-in closet like in the United States), so I could cry. It was too much for me, especially, when all of our reacquired possessions were marked for auction, and we were told we had to move. Because we had a phone, I think my mother applied for post-war help which were rentals in Hamburg where they were building huge apartment blocks. We qualified and moved to Hamburg into a high rise apartment on the third floor. We moved in the first of May 1952. My brother Harry had received money and a passport to America from my grandmother. He left the second of May on the ship, MS *Italia*, for New York. I think he was a cabin boy. I left three weeks later on May 22, 1952, when the boat returned. I was fifteen years old, almost sixteen, and very undernourished. The only reason we could leave was because the war was over, and the fact that my father had been born an American in Harlem, New York. My mother never said good-bye to me because my grandparents helped me get to America.

Brother Harry waving on the MS Italia when he left Germany to go to America 1952

Harry was eighteen, but because of the war time, they issued him a passport even though the rule was five years before your twenty-first birthday you had to leave. The United States Consulate in Germany made exceptions because of the war. That is why I left at fifteen, almost sixteen. No dual citizenship was allowed at that time.

COMING TO AMERICA

On Board the Ship MS *Italia* and Arriving in New York

The MS *Italia* was like the *Queen Elizabeth* except it had only two stacks instead of three. I stayed in an inside, downstairs cabin way at the bottom. I had a little suitcase with a set of clothes. There were three other ladies in my cabin, if I remember correctly. I didn't know much about them because all of us left early to go to work. I worked in the nursery on board ship. It was an eleven-day trip one way from Hamburg, Germany, to New York. Many people became seasick, but I did not. I enjoyed the wonderful food on the ship and learned a few English words, but I also got my first period and didn't know anything about that because no one had ever told me about those things.

Our first stop was in Halifax, Nova Scotia. This was where many of the families immigrating to Canada got off the boat.

Cruising down the channel to New York City was the most anticipated moment. Everyone was standing by the railings in the front and sides of the ship. It was about seven in the morning. There was the beautiful clear weather and homes along the channel and people waving. The ship blew the whistle: the horns were very loud. We were all screaming, and I was overwhelmed to realize I didn't even know that America had a "*Statue of Liberty*" or high rises (this was before the Twin Towers were built). The Empire State Building took my breath away.

My anticipation was suddenly more of anxiety about my future and praying for the first time that I would be able to find my brother, Harry, in this huge city. I wondered what my life would be like.

The man who asked me to help him with his two little boys aboard ship was in awe as well, but he knew his sponsors, distant relatives in upstate New York, would meet him. I had taken care of his two little boys when his wife died of a ruptured appendix aboard the boat. He had graciously asked if I would go with him, so I didn't feel quite so alone in this enormous city. There were so many people waving and more boats sailing around as we got closer and closer toward all the skyscrapers. Then I could see people waving American flags and shouting welcome (I was proud because I had learned a little bit of English aboard ship). These were breath-taking memories mixed with some fear and lots of joy. We made it to America! It had the bluest sky I had ever seen.

My First Place in Upstate New York - Poughkeepsie

I moved to a farming area with the man (I can't remember his name) and his boys. They lived in a trailer home, and I lived in the farmhouse. The area was much like Jeetze except everything seemed so big to me. I spent a lot of energy walking from building to building. One night when I first arrived, we were eating peach ice cream and there was a sudden bad smell. It was the first time I had ever smelled skunk. I have never liked peach ice cream since.

The dad was just beginning his attempts to find a job, so I spent time exploring the area while watching his children. One day I wanted to make a phone call to home but picked up the phone, and all I heard was noise. When I tried to dial the number I knew, it never worked. When I asked the farmer lady, she looked at the number and shook her head no and that it couldn't be done. I felt isolated because I couldn't contact my family, but it helped when I went with the family once a week into town to grocery shop, go to a movie, an auction, or to a bar to eat.

One day Harry was supposed to visit me, but he didn't show up. He was driving up with a friend he had made after being in New York for one month. The friend let my brother drive. Along the highway was a rockslide, and my brother was driving too fast, and they hit the rocks. Apparently, he was killed instantly. We received a phone call, and the family took me to the hospital because he had been in a car accident. He had died from severe head injuries that made it difficult for me to recognize him. The people at the hospital handed me his suitcase and few belongings—the bloody clothes and his watch which showed the time of the crash.

I prayed to God. I was numb and lonely, and I cried at the drop of a hat. The Lutheran pastor in Poughkeepsie did the funeral service and the Lord's prayer in German. The family I was staying with and I broke down and cried uncontrollably. I sent a telegram to my mother in Germany on the day of Harry's death asking what she wanted me to do, but I never heard back. Later, I learned from my sister that my mom hated me and said it was all my fault. That was a time of sadness with the loss of a family member and no one from my family with me. I sobbed and cried but was fully aware that I had to, and can, move on with my life and dream .I was not aware of it at the time, but I now know that God was with me the whole time and guiding me.

Got Picked Up to Go to Staten Island - July 22, 1952

I believe the pastor from Poughkeepsie made the connection for me to go to the Lutheran World Federation in New York City and set me up with the German speaking social worker, Mimi Kolff. I wanted to learn more English and become a nurse. Mimi Kolff took me in as my temporary guardian when I was sixteen. Mimi was a retired social worker for the Lutheran World Federation and lived on Staten Island. She picked me up from New York City. We took the subway and then the Staten Island ferry to her beautiful, old, New England style home with its screened-in windows that would be replaced in winter (she told me this when I asked her why there were so many windows in the shed by the lawn mower because I would mow her lawn which was hard to mow because it sloped toward the water). There were porches front and back. The grounds were situated two blocks from the channel where ships came in and out.

I recall crying on Mimi's bedspread for hours because I didn't know what would happen to me. It was a very uncertain time in my life; however, Mimi taught me how to make apple and cherry pie which I had never seen before. She started to make me say things in English, and I cleaned for her. I asked questions about her life and her house. Mimi also helped me with sewing a dress.

I remember a few events that happened while I stayed there. Because I loved being close to the water and liked to swim, I decided to take a swim from Staten Island to Brooklyn through the channel. I was swimming alone and a red ship tried to get me because I wasn't allowed to swim through the channel, but I didn't understand them, so I kept going. When I got to Brooklyn, they took me to the Marine Police Station. They tried to explain, but I didn't understand, so they gave me a towel and an ice cream cone and took me back. It was a very hot July.

A few days later, a neighbor girl named Faith who was a friend of Mimi had her eighteenth birthday party, and I was invited. They had a pizza party, but there was no cake. I missed the cake because all birthdays were supposed to have cake. Faith had some older brothers and her parents being Catholic, prayed that if they could get a girl with the next pregnancy, they would always dress her in blue. I thought that was very weird. She only had blue clothes.

Mimi told me about an older couple. They were thirty-nine and forty-one and had been trying to adopt but were considered too old. Mimi said they might be interested in taking me in. They wanted to meet me first, so Mimi took me to the Targee Street Bakery and Television Repair Shop on Staten Island. I met George and Anna Ballweg. Anna's family owned the bakery and George had the TV repair shop next door. George knew some German but mostly we communicated by pointing, using single words and action. While there, I cleaned the display windows with a pink cleaner. I don't remember what it was called. It produced a white powder which was hard to get off. They watched how I worked that day and shortly after that first visit, I moved in with Anna and George at 185 Targee Street, and it would become my home for the next couple of years. Although not official, they became my "American Parents." George was very tall and quiet at first, but soon became used to having me ask constant questions, and he answered them very patiently. Anna was short and heavy, but had a heart even bigger. Anna had three older brothers and one sister. Anna's mother was very heavy (around 250 pounds) and didn't come down to the bakery. Their apartment was over the store. The bakery was right behind George's shop, and there was a deli beside it. I would bring a Kaiser roll from the bakery over to the deli, and they would put a slice of ham and cheese in it for my lunch at school.

The brothers were the bakers and worked at night in the big bakery in the back. Everything was made by hand in those days. Marie, the sister, was the cake decorator and did an awesome job. It was interesting to me that my brother in Germany was an apprentice baker at the time. Bill was the oldest of the brothers, then Charlie, and then Albert. Albert was the only one who had a car and could drive. George got his driver's license and bought a Jeep in 1958 when they purchased a sixteen-acre property in New Jersey.

I recall a story while I was living there. I remember I went to the five-and-dime store once in a while with my friend to have ice cream shakes. I liked to buy postcards to send to my brothers and sister. I wrote occasional letters to my family and Marianne, my school friend. Local postage was three cents at the time.

The Ballwegs knew I wanted to go to school. George took me to Curtis High School, and I interviewed with a German teacher who became my advisor. He set me up to take English I and V and history, Physical Education, mathematics, and chemistry. I had only gone to school a part of sixth grade and still spoke mostly German, some Russian, and very little English. It was a full curriculum and was difficult to understand because of the language barrier.

27

My schedule during this time included working in the bakery by opening each morning at 5:00 a.m. until 7:45 a.m., and then I caught the bus to school. From 5 p.m. to midnight, I worked in the bakery. Between customers I could do homework.

I made three very good girlfriends, Joan, Alex, and Leta. Joan and Alex rode the bus with me at 7:50 a.m. each day. Alex spoke Russian and that bonded our relationship, and Joan lived a block down the street. These and other friends helped me find my way around the school, understand the schedule, and know where to go and get there fast before the next bell rang. I remember that all the children at school were very nice to me and would help me by answering all my dumb questions.

George had the patience of a saint. He would help with homework. I hated European history because I argued that what they were teaching was incorrect. He finally told me that I had to learn it that way to pass the class. My spoken English was pretty good. I flunked English I (the grammar stuff) but passed English V (writing and book reports.) Math and chemistry were a breeze for me, but I barely passed history. I received an "A" in Physical Education because I got to swim. In summer school, I retook English and German for more credits. High School was hard, but I finished it the next year and passed all the New York Regent Exams and graduated.

I remember a few things while living there. One of them was that as a child, I had experienced hunger. While working in the bakery, I was instructed to throw food away (all whipped cream cakes), so I ate as much as I could manage and gained weight (from the 103 pounds I started with to 148 pounds.) Another thing I remember was that I watched *Gunsmoke* on a small TV screen in a big cabinet in the bakery; it helped me to learn spoken English better.

I went to church every Sunday with George (deacon in church and usher at the 8 a.m. service) at Trinity Lutheran. I sang in the choir. On Mondays the bakery was always closed, so I would go for choir practice.

Pastor Carl Sutter of the Trinity Lutheran Church became my legal guardian. He was my confidant when I felt discouraged and helped with any questions I had. I never saw the pastor's wife or was invited to his home. Pastor Sutter's father was also a pastor and seemed quite old to me. Pastor Sutter's father would preach once a month, and he was a very good communicator, but he could get long-winded and one of the elders would usually cut him off after twenty minutes.

Trinity was a big church and had a full-time music director who led the choir and played the organ. I sang from the balcony in the big Gothic Church and that made it hard for me to really worship. I didn't feel like God was really present in my life. I enjoyed the choir members and spending time with them at practice, but never really made friends with them. In the summer, we had a barbecue in one of the church member's home and at Christmas time was another party. I attended, but I was the youngest member and never felt comfortable with the group.

After High School - Going to New York City

Anna and George were nervous when I decided to go to New York City but encouraged me to apply for a job. I worked at AT&T (American Telephone and Telegraph Company) on 185 Broadway as a typist, collator, and proofreader, but I didn't like sitting in an office; that just wasn't my dream. I applied to six nursing schools in New York City and Brooklyn. I lived in the YWCA on Fourteenth Street for the summer and while working there, George helped me find the nursing schools to which I applied. My grades were not the best, so I feared I may not be accepted but had good references from some of my teachers and Pastor Sutter about my work ethics. I prayed that it would help. I was accepted at the Norwegian Lutheran Medical Center in Brooklyn which was one of the smaller nursing and teaching hospitals for medical interns, residents, and nurses. I took a taxi for five dollars from the YWCA to the Norwegian Lutheran Home and Hospital (NLHH) in Brooklyn the day after Labor Day in 1954. I had two suitcases and some boxes and moved into the nursing school dormitory and had one roommate. I was there for three years. It was hard but wonderful, and I loved every minute of it. It was easier than high school. I was learning what I had yearned for all my life to know—how to help sick people get well or, if not, comfort them.

In 1957 or 1958, the hospital became the Lutheran Medical Center. When I arrived some of the Norwegian nuns were still working there. They lived in an attached building with other nuns. Some were teachers, and there were others who lived there but were too old to work. In the home for the nuns, there was a small one-keyboard organ, and we could use it whenever we wanted. It was like a parlor, and the nuns lived on the other side of the room. On weekends, I would play hymns one-handed and sing for a while. I was no pianist, but I could read notes and loved to sing.

The hospital's ground floor contained a piano. Vera was very good on the piano, and the nurses who weren't working on a floor would come after dinner and sing hymns and songs. There was an atrium from the ground floor which was open in the center all the way to the third floor. The ambulant patients would stand at the railings and some would sing along. Some of my favorite hymns were: "What a Friend We Have in Jesus," "Blessed Assurance Jesus Is Mine," "How Great Thou Art," "Just as I Am," and "I Walk in the Garden Alone." That was always the highlight of my day before returning to my dormitory to study. The lights were out by ten.

The rooms within the dormitory contained a small kitchen. I remember us making buttered cinnamon toast with sugar on white bread and toasting it in the oven. It was a yummy snack for us. There was one bathtub on the floor and several toilet stalls and sinks. There were no separate showers and about sixteen girls on a floor. In our room was a desk by the window, a very small closet, single bed, and a nightstand. We were expected to make our beds every day, and the sheets were laundered every week. We put the dirty ones in a bin outside in the hall.

Downstairs there were two classrooms where we had orientation and the instructors told us what was expected of each student. There were rules we had to live by such as no smoking, or bad language, no men or boys in the dormitory, and no dating until the last year of school. The house mother lived on the ground floor and did her rounds every morning and evening. Of course, it was lights out at ten at night. There was a small elevator (6' x 6') in which you had to close a skeleton door after the main door. I avoided it unless I carried lots of books.

I recall a few activities while I stayed, learned, and worked there. I was often the only one who stayed at the dorm during weekends. The others went home to their families and to mom's cooking. I thought the cafeteria food was great, and sometimes, I would treat myself to a bottle (6oz) of Coke from the machine, and sometimes walked Fifth Avenue, and looked in store windows. I did some shopping because, although the school provided the uniforms, I needed white stockings and shoes, and other necessities.

A tragic event happened fairly early in my training to become a nurse. In the early morning hours, my roommate said she could not get up. I said, jokingly, that I didn't feel like getting up either. It turned out that the girl had contracted bulbar polio and died six days later in an iron lung. All my fellow student nurses and I were devastated and had to get gamma globulin in each cheek to keep us from getting it. For me the dose was 30 cc in each cheek because the dosage was given according to your weight, but it was thick serum and hurt like crazy, and I could hardly walk. I couldn't lie on my back. I felt this was another test in life for me. Because I lost my roommate, I would go to the other rooms to talk and study. I needed others to help me get over the loss of my roommate and pray with me. God seemed so far away.

There were hospital rules for worship. We had to attend church every Sunday, even if we were working. There were four different Lutheran churches on Fourth Avenue. There were different times, morning and evening, and various Synods to choose from, so there was no excuse for not attending.

MY WORKING YEARS BEFORE MARRIAGE

Lutheran Medical Center

The hospital owned all the property on Forty-Fifth Street between Fourth and Third Avenues. They ran out of space and the Obstetrics and Gynecology Unit was in a separate building on Fifty-Second Street.

We had a medical ward with ten beds for women patients and a women's ward for surgical patients on one side of the building and similar wards for men on the other side of the building. When you were assigned to different floors all the time and were expected to be in charge, you really had to be on top of things. There were usually two students, one nurse (who was a senior nursing student), aides, and orderlies who did the lifting and often answered the call buttons. Between patients where white curtains to give privacy. Also, there were two floors with semi-private rooms for people who could afford to pay for them.

At the front of the wards were four beds for the more critical patients. Each patient was given a wash basin to wash their face and brush their teeth before bedtime, and each patient got a backrub with lotion. That was the time you got to know your patients and let them share their lives and feelings. Some asked questions we could not answer. In those days, we were not even allowed to tell them what pill or shot we were administering. The pat answer was, "You need to ask your doctor."

In those days, nurses did the care that aides and certified nursing assistants (CNAs) do today (take temps, blood pressure and pulse, and give baths). Nurses gave the medication sand injections. We had interns and residents to start IVs, and they got called for emergencies. Many of our interns and residents came from the Philippines and Japan.

In the surrounding area of the hospital in Brooklyn, there were many street fights. Each street seemed to be owned by a different nationality: Third Street was for the Spanish speaking people; Fifth Street was for the Italian people; and Eighth Street was for the Norwegian people. I bring this up because the hospital had to deal with the consequences of those fights in the Emergency Room. Most weren't serious like stabbings, but there were no shootings at the time.

After six months, there was a capping ceremony. If your grades weren't good enough, you were through and left at this time. We got not only our cap but, also our official white, heavily starched uniform aprons. It was good thing the hospital did the washing and ironing of all the uniforms!

Me in my full nurse's uniform 1954

My guardian, Pastor Carl Sutter from Staten Island, attended the ceremony and gave me a bunch of beautiful roses. I'm in the front and center of the class picture. I wasn't really special but had special people in my life.

Capping Ceremony at Lutheran Medical Center 1954

After the Capping Ceremony, there were classes for six hours and then I spent four hours practicing the skills I learned. Soon, I was assigned two or three patients to care for in the mornings and had classes in the afternoons.

In the second year of nursing school, I had a full eight-hour shift on the floor and eight hours of classes. We attended Brooklyn College for physics and chemistry. Things were trying at times and expectations were high. Sometimes those of us who worked the 4-12 shift like I did, would go to the nearby pizza parlor and sit and drink Coke and eat pizza. It was a place to vent stories and frustrations among my classmates. One of the things that happened to me during this year, while working on the semi-private wards, was that I saw a person falling from the upper story past the window on my floor. No one believed me, but they finally checked and found a dead patient in the street. I never forgot about that—ever.

I remember when I worked the midnight-to-eight morning shift that we not only answered the calls but had to make rounds on all the patients every hour. I had to hold the flashlight against my uniform so the light would not wake them up. During this shift, we would also wash, dry, and package rubber gloves (one to each side in a paper envelope), then sterilize them in an autoclave, and finally, put a sticker on it to notate that the gloves were sterile. There was no prepackaging and one-time use like there is today. We boiled catheters, rectal tubes, washed syringes, and sharpened needles for use the next day. Penicillin was the antibiotic of choice, and it was thick and white and would stick in the syringes. It also hurt the patients more than the newer drugs and intravenous drugs.

Another memory is our six weeks in Rockland State Hospital where we went for psychiatric training. It was in upstate New York and was a big complex of buildings. We had to carry a chain with a key around our waists as all the buildings were connected by underground tunnels. A couple of memories from that time stick in my mind. On the men's floor, there was a priest who was a homosexual and was busy studying to become an ophthalmologist. He knew he would never been reinstalled as a priest.

On the pediatric floor was a little three-year-old girl who was just rocking back and forth. Her diagnosis was schizophrenia. Her diagnosis was common at the time because they didn't have diagnoses such as attention deficit disorder, or oppositional defiant disorder, autism, and the like. I took her and put her on my lap and started signing to her in German. She looked at me surprised and started singing with me. Her nurse told me she had not said a word or made a sound since she arrived. She was apparently raised by a Jewish grandmother. Sadly, we left and I don't know what happened to her.

In our senior year (the third year), we completed all classes and had to fill in our skills lists. We took charge of the floors and were assigned regular schedules. I liked the 4-12 shift because we were able to be in charge of our floors but were assigned different floors.

I earned some income by working the hospital switchboard some weekends. I plugged in each phone to another phone using the switchboard. I knew all the gossip in the hospital because if there was no background noise, I could listen in on which doctor was flirting with which nurse and so on. At nights, I took calls for C-sections in the operating room or on Fifty-Second Street, seven blocks away which was the hospital's maternity building because the main hospital wasn't big enough. I received fifty dollars for each case and it paid for my education. Babysitting only paid three to five dollars, and I was saving money to go back to Germany.

During this year, I was mostly assigned to the pediatric floor which was the specialty that I wanted. This was the most difficult area for most students, but it was my favorite. We had all kind of specialties in pediatrics such as medical, surgical, orthopedic, and cancer. The tonsils and adenoids cases stayed one night for fear of bleeding. The most heart-breaking were the burn cases and the children with cancer. There was really no treatment for that at the time. The hospitals had very strict visiting hours in those years— only two to three hours a day on Wednesdays and Sundays. On the pediatric floor, those children with cancer became my special patients. Some I had for several months, and one of them was Eugene.

Eugene was about two and a half years old and was diagnosed with leukemia the first time he came into the hospital. He was the only child of this Italian family and spoke his native language and English perfectly. He spent most of his time with adults. It was when he was almost three when he was admitted again, and he looked very pale and had no energy. He needed a blood transfusion. I had him as my patient on the 4-12 shift, and he became sort of my favorite. Because of the restricted visiting hours, his parents only came from two-to-four on Wednesdays and Sundays. His dad did not come up to see him because his mom said he couldn't handle seeing all those sick children, so we waved to him from the window. Eugene never complained to his mother when she was there because he didn't want to upset her. After she left, he would come to me and say, "Miss Struckmeyer, I really need something for pain." Then, he would start to cry. He was such a brave boy. I just loved him and often held him on my lap while charting. After he died, I went to the funeral parlor to comfort his large family. He was the only offspring of the whole clan. I remember his mom coming up to me while I was standing by the casket and while crying, she said, "Doesn't he look peaceful?" I wanted to say, no, he looks dead but held my tongue.

There were so many sad cases and so few cures for cancer at the time, but I gave the kids what I could for pain, love, and comfort, and they loved it when I sang German lullabies to them.

The hardest cases for me were the burn cases. We had a little girl, I think she was five years old, who was wearing this beautiful (nylon?) dress on Sunday for church. Apparently, the brother was playing with a cigarette lighter or a candle on the table in the house. Her dress caught on fire, and sixty-five percent of her body was covered with third degree burns. There were no burn centers in 1956. Taking care of her with the intern and the residents and changing her dressings just about tore out my heart. It took a good three to four hours of pain and screaming. She was isolated, so she was not only in pain, but was lonely and scared. Her parents could only wave through the window into the room if we pulled the curtain back.

Medicine has really changed, and I'm glad most children recover from childhood cancers. God always gave me the strength and love for the sickest children. At times, I had a hard time thinking why God allowed such things to happen and had trouble going to sleep. These were often times when I wondered about my belief in a good God and why my prayers for all those suffering children were not heard or answered. Was Jesus really listening to our prayers? We often talked about that when we sat down at the pizza parlor down the street after our midnight shifts. We never really came to a real answer—except to have more questions.

All patients stayed in the hospital for much longer times. For example, for a gallbladder removal the average stay was eight to ten days, and a C-section was ten days. Also, there was very little patient education. Thankfully, all that has changed now.

Billy Graham Crusade in New York City - 1955

While I was going to nursing school, Billy Graham came to New York City and did a six-week crusade. We were very tired from our duties and classes at the hospital, but many of the nursing students including me took the subway to where the crusade was taking place. My fellow nurses wanted to see what was going on with the volunteering and then they asked for

German translators, so I became a volunteer counselor for German speaking people who came forward and asked many questions about accepting Jesus into their lives. Many Germans are very hard to convince of the gospel because they are strong and think they can do everything on their own, but I shared my story about how I became a Christian and how Jesus was becoming more and more real to me because of my experience here. I was taught what to say about the gospel, but I mostly listened about what they had learned that day and how they felt about it. It was a little nerve wracking when I was working with a person and one or two were standing outside the door, and also knowing I had to get back on the train to go back to the hospital. People would break down and cry, and I didn't always know what to say and didn't understand all of it because of the language barrier but all understood that this man (Billy Graham) loved God and wanted them to love Him too. That was the strongest message they got. I started feeling more of God's love there by doing His work and seeing all those people who came forward at Billy Graham's invitation. God's love is not for when I die: it's for every day. Billy Graham had a way of saying things that make people ask the question, "What am I missing?" It always comes back to me about how great God's love is.

The crusade included a big choir which I joined the days I could be there. Music was a big part of my life and made me feel closer to God and feeling His love for me. Those moments changed my life. The awe I felt as a child flooded back to me. Now I understood what the songs were actually saying. There were so many committed Christians in one place praising God. It was so awesome and created goose bumps. It cemented my faith in the love of the gospel—not the law which commands obedience which I had learned from other people and places—but the love of God who loves us no matter what. We don't have to do anything to have Him love us more. I wasn't changed in who I was, still a perfectionist and punctual, or my personality, but it changed my thinking about the future.

Billy Graham taught the simple gospel. Romans 3:23 states "For all have sinned, and come short of the glory of God." I didn't really think that I was a sinner because I had done "so many good deeds." I was sure that God would know that and accept me into heaven.

John 3:16 stuck in my head. "For God so loved the world, that He gave his only begotten Son, that whosoever believes in Him, shall not perish, but have everlasting life," and John 14:6 where Jesus says, "I am the way, the truth, and the life: no man cometh unto the Father, but by me." I often reread the word of Paul on a plaque that someone had given me. The plaque said, "For me, to live, is Christ; and to die, is gain." I meditated on Philippians 4:4: "Rejoice in the Lord always, and again I say, Rejoice." From this I had the motivation to be cheerful even when I lost Eugene, the little boy I loved so much who died of cancer.

Graduation From Nursing School, a Job at a Pediatric Ward, and Returning to Germany

On September 6, 1957, I received my nursing degree (RN). I was twenty-one years old at the time. Many people came to my graduation.

I was hired as head nurse on our large pediatric ward as soon as I passed the Nursing State License exam. I loved the job with all the challenges. It paid $3.15 an hour, and I worked double shifts a lot. By November, I earned enough money to buy an airplane ticket to Germany and back.

In order for me to be able to go to Germany and come back to America, I was sworn in as a naturalized citizen of the United States of America in New York City. I had been in the USA five years and was twenty-one years old allowing me to get a permanent passport. In mid-December of 1957, I left for a vacation to Germany. It was not an easy decision to make because I was afraid that my German was rusty, and they would make fun of me, and they did, and that was okay because I really wanted to see my family. I was anxious to see my brothers and my sisters, and my parents. I wasn't sure how my family was doing because I had some pictures of my sisters who looked so emaciated as well as my mother. When Vati returned from jail, he wrote to me once a month, but I missed all the weddings except my youngest sister's. Mom was doing well because Dad was out of the army and working again as a lawyer.

After five years away and when I arrived, I was amazed at the rebuilding of Hamburg, seeing my parents doing so well, and my little sisters who were teenagers dancing to rock and roll on the radio for hours. I felt I had changed and life had really changed. I didn't feel I really belonged and was a foreign visitor. My sisters "stole" my beautiful clothes—I let them keep them. The girls were so grown up, healthy, and spoiled. They didn't have a lot of things because Germany was still recovering from the war. They had the necessities but not much more.

There were still a few places that were totally destroyed but mostly the buildings were rebuilt to look the same way as before the bombings, but inside they were different. There were no very high ceilings anymore.

They were more practical for heating and cooling. While walking and reacquainting myself with the area where my family still lived (the high rise building at 56 Grindelberg on the third floor), I noticed there was a horse butcher. I asked my sister, who was walking with me, and she said that it was quite common to eat horse because other meats were not available. I couldn't believe it. I don't think I ever ate it.

Renate and my three brothers outside of Grindelberg housing

There was definitely a wall between my mother and I. I respected my Mutti because she was my mother but did not feel love towards her even though I tried. I learned in the ten commandments that we are to honor our mother and father so that it may be well with me.

My mother took me to some areas of Germany which I hadn't seen. It was supposed to be a two week trip, but we were in a car accident between Heidelberg and Frankfurt. The car had a tire blowout on the right rear, and mother was driving too fast (130 km/hr or 80 mph). The car somersaulted, and I was thrown out the front windshield (no seatbelts in car). I was hit by an oncoming car and ended up in the hospital in Frankfurt for six weeks with a fractured pelvis, severe head injuries, road burn, and lacerations. I fell into a coma, then awoke after eleven days, and everything was a blur because my glasses were broken, and I couldn't see or remember much. My dad came and sat with me until I came around and then he had to go back to work.

I was overwhelmed with mail from the United States supporting me. The nurse couldn't believe it nor could my family. I worked hard at physical therapy to get strength back and the use of my right leg (foot drop and dragging). My father hoped I could stay but I said no; however, later in my recovery period, my dad took me and my mom to Heidelberg, Freiburg, Basel (Switzerland), and Munich. Southern Germany is so different from the big city I lived in. I really enjoyed being with my friends who lived in Freiburg. They showed me all around the Black Forest area in their car. I stayed with them for a week during my recovery.

Back to Lutheran Medical Center and on to United States Public Health Service Hospital (Veteran's Hospital)

I flew back to Brooklyn at the end of February after more than two months in Germany and started back to work at the Lutheran hospital for a few months and then moved back to Staten Island to live with the Ballwegs. I moved in with them and worked at the Veteran's Hospital. It was a difficult working environment. There were often two nurses and many male orderlies to give care. It was for WWII and Korean War Veterans (many had ulcers), and a cancer ward.

I was either the charge nurse who had to chart on all the patients (many of them you hardly saw), or I was the med nurse and handed out pills and shots all day. I was more used to the one-on-one care and doing everything for my patients, and knowing and understanding their needs.

I was transferred to the cancer ward which consisted of cancer of the eye, ear, nose, and throat area (everything from the neck up). From injuries sustained during the war, many of them had to have their faces put together and stitched up. There was cancer of the throat caused by smoking and what they inhaled during the war. The doctors had to remove the larynx, and they didn't have the artificial voice boxes they have today. I had to comfort people who had lost their eyes and were blind. It was overwhelming for one nurse to provide thirty or forty patients with medication. The VA hospital expected so much from nurses. They didn't keep a nurse for more than a month. I worked there about a year and was burned out.

The Bielefelds (the bakers) and the Ballwegs had purchased sixteen acres of land (eight acres was forest). The Bielefelds built their home there in Flemington, New Jersey. They sold the bakery and moved there. I followed them there after I resigned at the hospital. The Ballwegs sold their TV business a few years later and moved there, too. This was in the fall of 1960, and I had my own room in the Bielefeld's house. It was the smallest room, but I had what I needed. When I wrote my Vati in Germany about moving to Flemington, he bought me a little Opel Kadett car and then I could put my driver's license to use. Flemington was mostly a farming area, but it was famous for a porcelain factory, a glass factory, and the first ever "outlet" store. It is a beautiful area close to Philadelphia, Pennsylvania.

I worked at Huntington Medical Center at night. To get a job in nursing was pretty easy, but usually one had to start on the night (12-8) shift. I was assigned to a medical floor. After a while if someone left, you might get on the day shift. I was on the night shift for more than a year. It was hard because I had trouble sleeping during the day.

In April, I promised to chaperone the sixteenth birthday of Marianne, a relative of Anna's in Germany (daughter of Anna and George adopted the year after I came to live with them in 1952). She was six years old at the time.

I was sleep deprived from working several nights in a row and chaperoning a barbecue in the back woods and was sitting on a rope swing suspended from a high tree. While I was supervising, I dozed off and fell off the swing, and my arm was caught in the chain. I landed on the roots of a tree. I knew I had broken my wrist, but I held my arm very still for the rest of the party. I drove to the hospital by myself, and the pain was very bad, but I made it. My wrist, humerus, and clavicle were all broken. I was in a full arm cast and sling for two months and couldn't work.

I inquired about Lutheran Churches when I moved to Flemington and heard there was only one in the area. That was St. Paul's Lutheran Church. It was a mission church, so it was brand new, and it was extremely conservative during the time. The church's property was right next to the hospital where I was working. I became a member and then babysat for Pastor and Vi (short for Violet, I think) Opsahl. They had six boys and one girl at the end who was the youngest at the time.

My husband-to-be was interviewing people in the area to see if there were enough people who did not go to church and may be able to help new churches to grow. I helped Vi, the pastor's wife, with their seven children.

I also did mending, sewing, and ironing as well as helping with getting the vegetables cut and dinner ready. I also sang in the choir and practice was held in the basement of the parsonage. The fellowship hall at the church was not yet completed.

One Sunday in June when he was the guest preacher, a young seminarian named Manfred Berndt preached a sermon. He had a cute smile and a German accent. Pastor Opsahl told me that he was doing a summer vicarage for the Atlantic district and had broken up with a girl in Long Island and wanted nothing to do with girls. I invited him to have lunch at our house after church. He said that he loved to eat and would always accept a free meal. Manfred was only supposed to be in the area for two weeks, but due to the death of the assigning bishop, he was there for six weeks, and I like to say that was long enough to get him hooked. God showed His faithfulness at this time because He helped me find a great husband—a wonderful and caring man to know and love.

MANFRED BERNDT, OUR COURTSHIP, AND MARRIAGE

Manfred was handsome. He was blonde-haired and blue-eyed, about six feet tall, with broad shoulders, but more importantly, he was humble, he loved God, and he was a gentle man. He was physically fit because he was on the college and seminary tennis teams. In his youth, he was a soccer player in Argentina. Out of the ten children, he was the only one born in America, then he moved back to Argentina until he was thirteen when his parents decided to settle down in Wisconsin. He went to boarding high school in Milwaukee, Wisconsin, (Concordia Lutheran School), and after high school, he went to Concordia Lutheran College for four years and then on to Concordia Seminary in St. Louis, Missouri.

Seminary graduation picture of Manfred Berndt 1960

Our courtship from the time Manfred left for St. Louis to continue to study for a master's degree in theology was mainly through letters and very rare phone conversations. At Thanksgiving, he invited me to come with him to Wausau, Wisconsin, to meet his parents and family. I flew from Newark to St. Louis, and he met me at the airport with a friend's car he had borrowed. It was exciting to see him in person again. Together with three other young men, we piled into a car and drove to Wausau, actually, Wittenberg, Wisconsin, where his dad was a pastor. We arrived late that night, and I was nervous about meeting all his family. Actually, only two sisters and three brothers were there and his mom and dad. I was surprised by their acceptance of me and was sure it was because I was from German roots.

We did a lot of talking that weekend and took long walks for some shared time alone. Clearly, we became more and more aware of our likenesses and of our differences. I shared my concern about what my parents might say about me marrying a preacher. I had not yet told them of our relationship at all but knew I had to sooner or later. That weekend was a wonderful one, and Sunday we left for Milwaukee. I was supposed to fly out that day, but we had a bad snowstorm, and I was put up in a hotel for the night. I had to call New Jersey to let them know I wouldn't be back for work. It was a lonely night knowing Manfred and his friends were driving to St. Louis in bad weather and me left alone in a cold hotel room, but it was also a good time to ponder our relationship and to realize God's plan and faithfulness for our lives.

After getting back home and to my work routine, it filled each day, and each day I wrote a letter to Manfred and looked forward to receiving his. When none came, there was always a moment of disappointment but then the next day I received two or three letters that made up for it. On December 17, 1960, Pastor Opsahl and Vi invited me for dinner, and at the end, gave me a little package. It was an engagement ring from Manfred but no note. I was taken aback by the way I received it. There was no formal "will you marry me" until the letter then came to Opsahl's the next day explaining how they were supposed to give it to me for Christmas with an official request to marry him. The letter was supposed to come before the package.

Christmas seemed lonely without Manfred so far away, but a phone call was the balm to hold me over and besides it was my Christmas to work at the hospital.

We set the date for our wedding, and now all our letters were full of love and plans. When I told my parents about Manfred, my dad's reaction was, you are too young to marry a minister, and you won't have any fun in life with him. That remark only spurred me on to show my parents how loving and caring Manfred was and how much we can have together.

For Easter break, Manfred came to New Jersey and stayed with us in Flemington. We spent time addressing invitations, finalizing wedding and rehearsal plans, and just having time romancing and taking walks. We took drives in my "Opel," and before I knew it, he left me again with a promise that as soon as school was over, he would be back.

In early June my parents arrived on a ship from Germany, and I picked them up in New York. The next day, we took a ride in New Jersey, and I had an accident and totaled my car, only twelve days before the wedding. My parents weren't hurt, and I had a concussion and was in the hospital for a couple of days. My car was ruined, and I told Manfred I did it because I wanted to be sure he didn't marry me for my car.

We did have a nice visit when Manfred came for the wedding and went to show my parents around Washington, D.C., for a couple of days of sightseeing, and I could tell quickly how much they liked Manfred and thought I had made a good choice. Of course, I'm convinced that our meeting was arranged by God, or it just wouldn't have happened. Manfred who was born in the Midwest but moved with his family to Argentina, and me, from Germany and the East, should meet in Flemington, New Jersey, seems nearly impossible—but not for God. He can do all things and is so good to all His children.

The wedding day at St. Paul's Lutheran Church in Flemington on June 17, 1961, was hot and humid, but everything went perfectly as planned. My dad played the piano at the reception in the fellowship hall, and friends filled the church from New Jersey, and Queens, New York, where Manfred did his vicarage the year before, and from Staten Island, and Brooklyn— what a day!

Jutta and Manfred cutting the wedding cake— June 17,1961

Our honeymoon was a weekend in Stanhope, New Jersey, in a cabin by the lake. It was wonderful to have a couple of quiet days alone, but I also learned quickly that Manfred is not a procrastinator. We spent most our time writing "Thank You" notes knowing that we would be leaving for St. Louis and the mission school for six weeks in a couple of days. Manfred had received a call to be a missionary to Hong Kong. Six weeks of mission school was required, and I'm thankful for that. Also, we had to have physicals and all kinds of shots to make sure we were fit. We spent the next six weeks in an apartment near the seminary, and I found out how hot and humid St. Louis got in the summer. There was no air conditioning in the apartment.

I didn't consider myself to be a missionary at first, but we were going to St. Louis first for school. I never went to any Bible schools, and my knowledge of the word of God was limited to going to church on Sundays and doing morning devotions with "The Portals of Prayer" or similar booklets. I never looked much deeper since I was always working or studying for my nursing jobs.

Our car was packed to the brim, and when we arrived in the evening, driving on highway forty in Ohio, we suddenly had this weird sound in what we thought was the tire, so we drove very slowly with our hazard lights on to the next exit and the first gas station, a Sohio station. They were closed, but the owner lived next door. He offered us a room to stay for the night and fixed our car the next day. It was a bearing in the tire and was no problem. They happened to be Lutheran and felt sorry for us, I guess. God showed His love again.

When we got to St Louis, we had a little apartment—a bedroom upstairs, and a living room, and kitchen downstairs. It was furnished, and we only needed some kitchen stuff and bedding. It was no mansion but comfortable except for the humidity and heat. There was no air conditioning. Then it started-school every day, reports to write, research to do, but it was all fun. The anticipation of going into the field of mission work peaked my interest. There were physicals, inoculations of all sorts, physiological briefing, and homework. Manfred played tennis a couple of times a week.

Soon our passports and visas arrived and our flight to Hong Kong was as scheduled. We had a short layover in Hawaii for one weekend. We had a wonderful time seeing new sights like palm trees and flowers, and hearing new sounds of exotic birds. The sounds woke me up at the first sign of light and kept getting louder and louder. We walked the beaches and took a tour around the island.

HONG KONG

Arriving in Hong Kong - September 6, 1961

After a long, tiring flight, we finally arrived in Hong Kong, which had a small shed-like airport at the time. Several missionary families met us, and we stayed with George and Florence Winkler for the first two weeks until we found an apartment. Our arrival was a day before the arrival of our first typhoon. It was humid and hot and everything smelled musty to me. One of the families, the Holts, had seven little boys. All of them had their heads shaven and were painted with gentian violet for impetigo which is a contagious, superficial skin infection caused by Staphylococcus bacteria. They looked awful. I said to Manfred that first night, if we stay here, I refuse to have children.

During this term, we moved into an apartment on Suffolk Road. Our apartment only had two bedrooms, and Manfred used the small one as an office. We divided the larger one into two bedrooms making use of every inch of space with a storage closet built into the top near the very high ceilings. Everyone was very good to us and as soon as we got our own apartment and bought some furniture and were sort of settled in, we started our private language study of Cantonese with Mr. Wong. He came every morning at 8:30 a.m. until lunch at noon, and we resumed our studies at

1:00 p.m. to 3:00 or 4:00 p.m. for two years, six days a week, to teach us to speak and write in Cantonese. For me, it was more related to daily language you need in the market and at home with our part-time maid, A-Fong, and other people speaking Cantonese. For Manfred, it was more the language he would need with the leaders of the Hong Kong Church and Seminary. We had homework, and were expected to go into the market places and try out what we learned. It was hard work, but, at least, it was something we did together. Many times I had to use the English Dictionary to look at words I didn't know in English such as omnipresent, omniscient, Eucharist, and so forth.

Mr. Wong was not a Christian when he first came to us, but he had taught other missionaries before us. He was not a big man but pretty average in size and never talked about his family. He was always pulling the hair on his chin. The hair pulling was a weird memory I have about him, but after two years of language study with him, he helped me write my speech (a Bible study, lecture style) for a LWML (Lutheran Women's Missionary League) women's convention for Chinese Christian ladies.

My topic was on the women of the Bible. I did my research and wrote it up in English, and with the help of Mr. Wong, I translated it into Cantonese. Being an organizer, I had it done in plenty of time to memorize the six, long pages it took. I said it in the bathtub, in the car when driving, or recited it quietly in my mind over and over again. Then, came the day I was to present this. It was outdoors in one of the church's courtyards. I was on the platform with all those expectant Chinese women smiling up at me. All of a sudden, they became a big blur, and I could not remember how to begin. Then, I saw Manfred in the back smiling encouragement at me, and I realized how he must feel every Sunday or at school assemblies.

I looked down at my notes and started talking as if I had been wound up going faster and faster and faster. I was nervous and wanted to get it done. Manfred tried to signal me to slow down, but I was afraid. If I slowed down, I wouldn't remember where I was, so I just kept going. At the end, it seemed so much easier, and I even noticed people's responses and understanding of what a big risk I had taken.

Cantonese is a very hard language to learn: it has nine tones, and if you use the wrong tone, it can mean something very different. It did make me appreciate the acceptance and love these women showed me and the trust they had in me. God showed me His love in these women. God was faithful, again. It reminds me now how in Philippians 4:13 it says, "I can do all things through Him who gives me strength."

Most of those ladies were older, long-term missionary women who ran a craft store in an apartment and did Bible studies while people were making the items for sale. Some of those wonderful women were missionaries in China before the doors to China were closed to everyone, including Chinese people.

A-Fong was our part-time amah (maid) three days a week for all of our sixteen years in Hong Kong. She was a sole provider for her four children and alcoholic husband who lived in the slums at the time she started working for us. She was just five feet tall but a very hard worker. When we went on furloughs (time off and away from China), she took temporary work but always came back to us. She loved our children, Margarete and Dorothy, when they were born a few years later in Hong Kong on our first tour there in the early sixties, and often worked with a baby on her back. She would teach me to cook at least once in a while and usually bought food at the market place on her way to the house. She patiently corrected my bad Cantonese by restating it correctly. That was a big help to me to learn and helped me speak more correctly. Also, I taught some women to speak English.

In February, I got pregnant with our first daughter, and I was sick all the time. During language study, I kept getting up to throw up. Also, I wasn't sleeping because of the mosquitoes and the heat and humidity. We finally decided to buy a window unit air conditioner. All the missionaries made fun of us thinking these new spoiled youngsters couldn't handle anything, but we ignored it. Soon they saw the difference it made in how I looked and felt because I could sleep at night, and before long, everyone had air conditioners in their bedrooms.

Due to my accident in Germany were I had a broken pelvis, the doctors at that time told me that if I ever gave birth to children it would have to be by C-section. I hardly remembered that or took it seriously because I was so young at the time. When I became pregnant with my first child, Margarete, that memory returned, and my doctor who took care of me for my prenatal visits confirmed the fact, so my time to have the surgery was scheduled early. On the scheduled date, I went to the small hospital run by a Catholic organization, and my doctor was an American general physician. He had not done a C-section since medical school, but read up on it. He was ready and was there on the scheduled day in the operating room.

Because no anesthesiologist was available there, we decided to have spinal anesthesia. They gave me my spinal anesthetic and within seconds, I had the worst headache I ever had. I thought the top of my head had blown off. They checked my blood pressure. They said it was so high that it didn't register at the top and the bottom was over 160 mmHg. I thought I was going to die. We said prayers together with Manfred by my side.

Since I was in a Catholic hospital, the nuns who were the nurses in the room were praying with their rosary beads. I could see out of the corner of my eyes since I was still lying on my side. The assistant doctor who did the spinal tap tried to draw out some fluid, but my doctor yelled, "We need to get the baby out!"

That is the last I remembered until I was in my room and saw Manfred. My first question was, "Is the baby all right, and was it a boy or girl?" Then I said to Manfred, that he would never come near me again. He looked white and totally drained by the experience. Manfred prayed and cried and said, "God saved you because the baby and I need you so much."- God is good, always, as I realized that truth.

After I had Margarete in November 1962 and survived the traumatic experience that might have ended my life, I became more involved in wanting to know more of the whole story of the Bible and read as much as I could and asked many questions. I thought just to know I was baptized and confirmed was enough. When Margarete was baptized, I was overwhelmed with God's grace for me since I know I had almost lost my life having her. I got goose bumps all over. God took care of me without me ever asking. It was just another wonderful, unexpected miracle. What a time it was to grow closer to understanding God's grace!

About China and Our Work There

China closed its doors to people and any Chinese outside of the country and the engagement of commerce with other countries in 1949. A few of the old time missionaries who came from China after the doors closed to that country started Bible studies for women who lived in tents with families. Many had tuberculosis and were treated in the temporary clinics in Rennie's Mill which is located on a half island which is attached to Hong Kong. They built a chapel and a small hospital there, and when I arrived in 1961, I did some help with teaching nurses there. Also, these women started a handicraft center, and the women and children started making various items that were then sold to get money for more materials needed for what they made. Many of the Chinese women were very talented and could come up with new crafts to make. All had great ideas and worked hard. They worked in groups while one of the missionaries would lead Bible studies for them. There were also many men that had no place to go and pastors had Bible studies with these men. That started the mission to grow. Several of those men who were in Bible study became pastors after many years.

By the end of 1968, many of the business executives in Hong Kong and other Americans living there approached the Hong Kong Synod of the church to open an American (not British) school for the expatriates. After canvassing all the high rises in Repulse Bay, Hong Kong Island, it was clear that there was more work to be done. I was one of the people who helped with the canvassing for several weeks. What a joy to get to know people who spoke English again!

During our sixteen years there, we opened six new schools and churches for Chinese speaking people and students. Some of the churches were in apartments on the first floor (not the ground floor) of business buildings and some were on the roofs of the housing built by the government for refugees. They were usually brick buildings in the shape of an "H" with the center for the bathrooms and staircases. Each apartment was just an eight-by-ten room. There were no kitchens, so everyone cooked in front of their doors. The rooftop schools were usually primary schools.

Where We Lived

We lived in Kowloon Tong on the mainland and worked with people who spoke Cantonese. Our first Christmas season in Kowloon was the hardest time for me. Asking what it was like from the other wives of missionaries did not prepare me for the shock. We put up a small fake tree and decorated it. Before Christmas, students from the schools came in big groups to see the customs we had on the holiday. We baked so many different cookies because they came to sing Christmas carols. In previous years, the Chinese students were used to coming to see the missionaries' houses and marched around the table. They received goodies from us after singing Christmas carols in Chinese. I was not used to this after only four months in Hong Kong and found it uncomfortable to be so invaded. After they left, I just cried as Manfred and I sat around our Advent candles to do devotions and sing carols in German and English. I missed my family really bad for the first time in all the years since I left home in 1952. I still loved the German Christmas carols best, and Manfred tried to cheer me up by singing them with me and playing the piano. As we sang that helped a little, but still I felt empty and sad. Most of the holidays I spent with the Ballwegs and Bielefelds, and as a nurse, I always volunteered to work to let others go home to families. I still felt I didn't really belong there and God seemed far away.

Eventually I began to see that Hong Kong was a wonderful, busy place. Manfred was busy with churches and seminary.

Manfred's first sermon in Cantonese in Hong Kong 1963

In 1969, he even became the President of the Seminary until we left Hong Kong in 1977 to go back to the United States.

I stayed at home and took care of Margarete when she was born and practiced my Chinese on A-Fong. She would act like she didn't know what I was saying, and then repeat the sentence with what I should have said. Another child, Dorothy, came along, and our schedule got busier and busier. I spent time with friends who had children of similar ages and went to the club (the British Club-the USRC) to go swimming in the hot afternoons while Manfred worked or taught classes.

A Friend I Visited While in Hong Kong

My friend Virginia (Ginny) from nursing school married a Baptist minister right after graduation. They ended up becoming missionaries to Thailand. They were stationed way north in Chiang Mai close to the border of Burma (Myanmar, today). When Margarete was about six months old, we decided to go visit my friends there. We flew a smaller plane to Bangkok and were typical tourists for a couple of days. We did some shopping in a boat on the river which was like the shopping area of the city. Then, we flew in an even smaller plane to Chiang Mai which has no paved road and oxen walking down the main street (a very primitive area even now). The temperature was just a bit lower than Hong Kong or Bangkok being further north. There was simple housing and few conveniences. The mission did supply some better housing but with very erratic electric supply, it was still a hard place to live for spoiled Americans. The language was similar to Cantonese but also hard to learn. I learned how to say "How are you?" after five days there ("Sava di ih ka?"), or something like that, and "Nei ho ma" in Cantonese.

The churches had no walls and low benches. It was pretty full on Sunday and there was very lively singing. It made me appreciate what they were doing, bringing the love of Jesus to that land. Also, I was aware again that we were so blessed to have been sent to Hong Kong by God, instead of Chiang Mai. My prayer for them and all the missionaries increased, and every day I thanked God for them and other people sent by God.

Another blessing God gave me comes to mind. An amah (maid), who served the Spanish couple living in the house in front of our place, lived in a small room built for servants by our home. One early morning about five o'clock, I heard someone knocking on our window in the bedroom. I woke up to see what was going on. There stood the amah holding her very pregnant stomach. She was in labor. I woke Manfred and grabbed my bathrobe and was going to take her to the hospital. We got as far as out of the gate and to the Volkswagen Bug, and she got into the back seat and screamed. I checked, and the baby's head was showing. With her next pain, I delivered a healthy, baby girl. I quickly wrapped her in my bathrobe and laid her on the mom's stomach and drove to the hospital. The main gates were closed, and I had to ring a bell and share my predicament. She was then admitted, and I went home. My car was a mess. Soon her husband came and told us they named her Dawn. He also shared that they had lost a baby a few years earlier who died because of a sudden quick birth. I was so thankful for my nurse's training and thanked God for bringing them a live baby girl. That was quite a blessing for all of us. She sometimes brought Dawn to visit me at the house, and we shared how wonderful God was to let her enjoy her beautiful baby girl. I was sad that I lost touch with them after we went on our first furlough.

A Trip to Lantau Island

When Margarete was eight months old in August 1963, we had a vacation to Lantau Island[1] (*see appendix for map of area*) where a group of missionaries had a place up on top of the mountain. We did not take Margarete because we had never been there before and were told it was a very hard hike, and we wanted to see what the place was like. A-Fong took care of Margarete.

Chinese people carried the supplies needed. There were quite a few stone houses and a dining hall in the center of the little village. Each house had a small kitchen, bathroom, and two bedrooms. It was furnished with the basics. There were a lot of daddy-long-leg spiders, but was otherwise clean. There was also a swimming pool. Early in the mornings, you were almost always in the clouds because of the high elevation and the cool morning temperature. The later morning temperatures rose and the sun eventually lifted the clouds. We stayed only one night and then hiked back down and went on the ferry to take us back to Kowloon. In later years, we went with the whole family a few times. I write about the first time because coming back down, I felt really sick to my stomach and thought it might be a gallbladder attack because in school I learned that the women who most often got problems with gallbladder were female, fat and forty, and I was only twenty-six at the time. I found out later on that I was pregnant.

My second child, Dorothy, was born in April without complications in the new Baptist hospital with general anesthesia. On the second day, because this hospital had food service, I ordered hot oatmeal for the morning's breakfast. When it came, I noticed it was cooked in peanut oil and the oil was floating on the top; it was gross! I couldn't eat it and cried because I was so hungry. I called Manfred, and he called Florence, a missionary's wife who was taking care of Margarete. She brought me food that I could eat. I thanked God for a beautiful healthy baby girl, but in those days, I had to stay in the hospital for ten days, which by today's standards sounds ridiculous.

Another time we went to Lantau, when Richard was two years old, and it was the year of the first landing on the moon in 1969. One of the single missionary ladies brought her guitar, and we all (maybe, twenty people) prayed for the landing on the moon and sang for almost two hours. It was a joy to see and get to know the people from other denominations. It always renewed my love for Jesus, and my children loved being up there after they got used to the spiders.

Other Trips While Living in Hong Kong

One year after my three children got older, one of Manfred's cousins came to teach high school at the Hong Kong Lutheran International School in Repulse Bay on Hong Kong Island for a few years. She wanted to go to the Philippines for a visit during one of the school's breaks. I think it was in December because it wasn't that hot anymore. She didn't want to go alone, so Manfred encouraged me to accompany her, and I was excited to go there myself. Many missionaries had stayed with us on their return to the States, and they seemed happy and loved the country and the people in the Philippines, so when we flew into Manila we stayed in a missionary's home while they were gone. We spent two days in Manila before we took the bus to go to Baguio City because we wanted to go to Baguio City where it is supposed to be beautiful.

What impressed me in Manila was how colorful the city was. All the cars and busses were painted in cheerful colors. The taxis were mostly three-wheeled cars that just nosed their way into traffic even using the sidewalks as needed. Between cars, bicycles, rickshaws, and the busses, the pedestrians really were always in danger. At the restaurants people spoke pretty good English. It was just stressful to even get there while walking.

We slept well that night and were ready for our adventure taking the bus early the next morning. We talked to the neighbor, another pastor, and he explained how and where to get bus tickets and advised us to get to the station real early, which we did. Wow! That was an experience. We had to push our way into the bus and did get two seats together. Pretty soon the bus was not only full, but between the seats on both sides, two more seats flipped up in the middle. There were chickens, pigs, and all kinds of baskets with food (vegetables and fruit) laying on the bottom of the bus. Luggage was tied down on the top of the bus. It was amazing, and people were hanging on the windows outside of the bus. It was a two-hour trip in this scary, rickety bus along the edge of the mountains. Most of the road was so narrow that no one could have passed on the other side except in a few places. We were so grateful when we arrived safely in Baguio City—a beautiful town with a very nice hotel. We thanked God over and over again for our protection from this hazardous trip. There was a nice, green, golf course, and the president of the country had a mansion up there in the mountains. Praise God our return trip was a flight out of Baguio back to Hong Kong. Many years later an earthquake destroyed the whole city!

Another memory I have was that Hong Kong often hosted the various pastors from the Southeastern Asian region. There were natives along with the missionaries as well. I often got to be the tourist guide. Once I took a pastor from New Guinea shopping because he only had sandals. Everyone had suits and shoes and socks. He wanted to buy real shoes, I was told. I took him to the department store. It has a ground floor and another two floors, and he had never seen an escalator (he called it "moving steps" in Pigeon English) and was nervous to go on it. I had Dorothy with me at the time, and he got on it and was so excited about the moving stairs after he got to the top. He wanted to go on the next one, too. Then he went down the two floors on the down escalator and did the whole routine two more times before we got to the shoe area. He bought a pair of shoes and socks and put them on. He did not like them because most of his life he walked barefoot. He looked funny walking in them.

Another time I took two pastors from St. Louis to Rennies Mill in the Volkswagon with Dorothy again. Margarete went to a private preschool at the time. These men wanted to see the mission still active in the area. Rennies Mill is at sea level, and it is a steep decline to go down. That was not a problem until we had to go back up. The car kept stalling. I finally had to make them walk up the road while I drove the car up. The one man was a big heavy-set gentleman. It was embarrassing, but they were grateful for the time I took them there.

Issues and Things I Noticed While Living in Hong Kong

Living in the tropics or subtropics like Hong Kong, we get used to the daily afternoon showers. In 1964 when Dorothy was a baby, we had experienced a severe drought in the Far East. We had to live with water restrictions. We got water every fourth day. We filled drums, the bathtub, and boiled water and put it in glass bottles and containers. We stored water everywhere. This lasted for a whole year and worked all right for me, but for the many people living in squatters, it was a real hardship. Since we used regular diapers, and I had two girls in diapers, that became a challenge. Since Dorothy was born in April during the drought, I trained her by holding her over the toilet three times a day for bowel movements, and that's how she learned how to go potty on the toilet. Margarete, however, was trained with diapers, so I couldn't train her that way.

There was a lot of construction going on to build housing for the many refugees from China. I was amazed to see that the scaffolding for these high buildings was all made with bamboo tied with rattan strings. The workers seemed to be quite at ease climbing up and down like monkeys. I never heard of any major accidents which amazed me.

The Hospitals in Hong Kong While We Were There

The hospitals in Hong Kong were very different from where I had served in America. There were British hospitals like Queen Elizabeth on Hong Kong Island that served the expatriates and was quite modern. But the other hospitals were quite different. Patients slept on straw mats on cots, and most of the time the families took care of them and cooked outside for their loved ones. Nurses did mostly treatments like dressing changes and catheters. They also did medications and monitored what the patients could eat. Nurse's aides served water and often there were more nurses than they needed, and that's why I couldn't be a nurse there. I would not want to displace local people. Bathrooms were at the end of the halls of the wards.

Patient education was non-existent or not understood. I was aware of that when an amah was sent to me from another missionary because she had thyroid surgery. She still had her original dressing in place. I took it off and saw she still had her stitches in place and it looked infected. Checking with her to see if she missed an appointment with the doctor, she said she never got any information as to what to do when she got discharged from the hospital.

There was also a young missionary wife from a Scandinavian country who was home after giving birth to her baby and was never shown how she should care for it. It was harder for people like her when they are so far from home and have no family to help them. I believe she was Swedish. She knew some broken English. She was very homesick and felt alone because there were not many missionaries from her country. We were blessed to have so many missionaries like Florence and George. She had an appointment in six weeks with her doctor. I explained the importance of nursing the baby and helped her start. No pre-made formulas were available at that time in the area and no internet to order it! We prayed together, and I often visited her. She was a great mother and learned fast. I seldom saw her again because soon after that we went on one of our furloughs, and she was no longer there when I returned.

Customs of the Chinese

Chinese New Year is the only day most of the labor workers had a day off. Every year is named after an animal and is repeated every twelve years. Manfred's birth year was a Boar. I was in the year of the Rat; Margarete, a tiger; Dorothy, a dragon; Richard, a sheep; and Michael, a dog. It always created a discussion if we fit those descriptions, and we laughed about them.

One of the strangest customs at the time we first arrived in Hong Kong was on their New Year's Eve. If someone had a debt that was unpaid, they had until midnight to pay up or there were serious consequences. One evening a man appeared at our house and needed to talk to Manfred. The next thing I knew, Manfred took the car keys and disappeared. He came back later and told me that he had to take him somewhere to stay where he could not be found because the Chinese man could not pay his debt. I don't know what would have happened to him otherwise. I never really understood that, but I was scared what might have been. I was glad Manfred was back safely. During that time, you also gave a gift of money to families and friends on New Year's Day in a small, fancy, little, red envelope. I learned I had to give one to A-Fong and the people to whom I was teaching English at my home.

In fall, the Full Moon Custom is celebrated by families parading around their neighborhoods with a fancy lantern lit, and singing Chinese songs. It is called the Lantern Festival, and the children all dress up, and I love it that our children always joined them and enjoyed the walk around the sports stadium. It is a very colorful time; the kids wear a lot of red costumes.

Our American Thanksgiving was celebrated only by the missionary families and friends. There was only one Thanksgiving service in one of the Christian churches and that rotated to other churches every year. When we lived in the mission house, I had about forty for dinner. Some of the other missionary's servants came there to help A-Fong prepare the side dishes, and I did two large turkeys, one in our oven and in the one upstairs. Manfred planned games and activities, and we all had so much fun. In alternating years, it was celebrated at Winkler's place on 32 Oxford Road. In 1967, Thanksgiving fell on Thursday the twenty-sixth, and I was scheduled for my cesarean section with Richard on the twenty-seventh. I was glad the Winkler's held the party at their place. After that year and most others, both Margarete and Richard ended up with candles on pumpkin pies for their birthdays. Halloween was not celebrated, so our children did not know much about that custom until we were in the States.

More About the Chinese People

To get to the Hong Kong Island, we had to take a ferry. I loved to sit in the ferry terminal called Tsim Sha Tsui watching people come and go. Often the locals dressed in warm jackets and carried children on their backs. Toddlers wore a lot of clothes on top including down jackets but nothing below (naked). This was very practical for people not spoiled like we were with fancy homes, washers and dryers, and an amah. The foreigners, especially the British people, wore sun dresses in the fall and winter.

Near our home on Oxford Road was a small, walled village called Kowloon City. It was known for crime. They had small alleys, not wide roads for cars, and they had their own kind of government. The Hong Kong people said it was off limits—even the police would not go in there. We had some church members there and their children went to Concordia Lutheran School. When Manfred and one of his pastoral students went there to visit a family, it was time for serious prayers for me and the girls. I guess daytime was not as dangerous because they were fine and returned safely.

*Second from the right is the Chinese lady who requested a cere-
mony, "discarding of the idols," at her house, which were four little altars, after she and her family became Christians.*

Most foreign visitors did their shopping in the big hotels. They were intimidated by the crowded streets. The ocean terminal had a big shopping mall inside and visitors would do a lot of shopping there. When I took visitors, Manfred and I would take them to the local street markets in the evenings to see the real everyday life of the local population and always warning them to watch their valuables. The pick pockets were very professional in their craft.

One time I took a few lawyers from Germany to the market. The ex-husband of my sister was the reason I knew them. It was spring time and close to the University's final exams. We saw some Chinese men in long black capes sitting around a table. A live monkey head was clamped in the center, and the top of his head was sliced off. They were eating the brain with chopsticks while the monkey was screaming. The lawyers could not believe that people actually believed that doing that would help them pass exams and make them smarter. Claus (one of the lawyers) said that he had nightmares about that. The markets have everything in them including food, fish, clothing, and gifts for every occasion. It was one of the ways to also practice my Cantonese language skills, and I learned much needed bargaining skills.

My Thyroidectomy and Depression

I think it was in the spring of 1972 that I had to have a thyroidectomy. It was my dentist who saw the growth in my neck and said I should have that checked out. After surgery, the sample of the tumor was sent to Japan for diagnosis and took several weeks for a return answer. It was early stage carcinoma, but they removed it all. When the thyroid was removed, my hormones went wacky and the doctor had to play with finding the right amount of medication, and it can take a long time. The problem I experienced was totally unexpected. I went into a deep depression. I could not get out of bed. I felt my neck was not strong enough to hold my head up. My doctor came to the house after Manfred told him what was going on and made an appointment for the depression with a psychiatrist. I was put on medications. The whole time I can hardly remember what went on. I feared God did not exist, and I was anxious when the children did not come home at the usual time, but really did not take care of them either. I walked around like a zombie. My dear friend, Traute, (*(a)see add.info.)*

was often by my side, and her amah came and cooked and cleaned on the days A-Fong was not there. I was scared, and I thought I was getting to be a drug addict. One on hand, I was always judging myself for being stupid and was empty of all feeling, and the next moment, I was anxious about life and the responsibilities I had. I feared I would be like my mother. I am thankful now that God was with me and helped put the right people in my life again. After almost a year, I think I was my old self again. I was off all the medication except the thyroid drugs. I now understand more clearly what people must feel when depression attacks them.

Visits From Relatives While Living in Hong Kong

In 1975, my parents came to visit us in Hong Kong for a few weeks. That was not an easy time. My dad wanted to see everything about the work we did in Hong Kong. Manfred took him to several places, and he was quite impressed by the work done everywhere in the schools, the seminary, and even the women's craft center. My mother just followed me around as if she was a puppy. I walked over to talk to my friends at 32 Oxford Road, and she stood by the gate just waiting for me with a cigarette in her hand. It was a good thing we had warm weather because I didn't want her to smoke in the house because it was a mission house.

After a few days translating in three languages, I got so confused and started speaking German to A-Fong and Cantonese to my parents. I prayed almost constantly for God to give me patience. They did bring the German language *Scrabble* game along for which I thanked God. At home in Germany, my mother did a lot of crossword puzzles in all the magazines and newspapers. She was very good at that, and if she was stuck on a question, my dad always seemed to know the answers. I have always loved to walk, but my mother doesn't ever go and made me feel like I was neglecting her if I went out. My dad loves to walk, but it's very slow but better than not at all. He would take my children with him on walks which was great.

Since my dad really paid close attention as Manfred patiently shared about the work of God in Hong Kong, I was hoping he might start to believe in God. Sadly, that did not happen; he told me, "That is for other people." I was praying a seed was planted, but when they went home, there was no one there to water it.

One funny memory of the visit is one Saturday Manfred took both parents for sightseeing in the morning. For lunch, I made German potato pancakes and fresh applesauce and bacon. Grinding so many potatoes by hand (almost six or more pounds) is hard work, but I made a whole, large platter full and kept them warm in the oven. As we were eating, my mom said she never makes them because it's too much work. They all ate well, and at the end, one was still on the platter and Manfred asked if anyone wanted the last one. No one answered, so he took it and ate it. My mother was mad at him later, and I asked what happened. She said she wanted the last one—crazy! Patience, Lord!

In 1976, my sister, Hannelore, visited in the early spring. It is not the best time to visit because the cold and high humidity can cause a lot of work. The inside walls in our large, living room and the bedrooms were all just whitewashed, and the water would run down the walls. In the bedrooms, we had window air conditioners but not the living room, so every morning you had to wash the walls to prevent mold. When Hannelore complained she was cold, I always had the pat answer, "You can wash windows and that would warm you up." The temperatures were not that low but with high humidity, it can seem cold and uncomfortable. She loved it when Manfred took her around. I think she believed in God, but they don't go to church in Germany.

My Job as a Teacher at the Baptist Church in Hong Kong

This is me teaching kindergarten at the Baptist church in Kowloon, Hong Kong 1973

When Michael turned three in April 1973, the Baptist Church asked me to run their preschool and kindergarten at one of their churches close to our area. I had gotten a teaching certificate from the Hong Kong University for teaching English and German at our Concordia school next to the seminary. This was all volunteer work, but I loved it so much. Well, this was going to be my first paid job for the first time since I got married. I was very nervous for the interview, but they were happy with me, and I got the job. I prayed that God would supply me with the wisdom to run this place. I loved and still love little children, but teaching them was very different. They had started with a few children the year before and had one teacher and an aide. The demand and list for children waiting to get in was long. I quickly learned how many children we could allow to come into each room. I tested the children, and they had to be able to know their colors and count to ten which was a requisite of the church. I quickly filled all the classrooms and added three new teachers and aides.

Since Hong Kong schools did not have kindergartens, it was easy to fill the four rooms because they allowed only twelve children in preschool and fifteen in kindergarten. The teachers were mostly the wives of missionaries or business executives. Three hours a day was all they wanted. Each teacher got a helper who was a Chinese lady who also spoke some English.

My job in the morning was to greet parents and often amahs who brought the children. All the teaching was in English. Once a season, we would have a day for a play we worked on and that was presented in the church upstairs for the parents. It was hard work for the teachers but fun to see the children grow. We had many various languages from different missionaries and locals, and all of them were learning English.

I did the daily opening in one room with all the children sitting on the floor. I used Bible stories from Concordia called "Arch Book" stories which were written for children, and I had ordered when my children were young. The pictures and stories were a big hit. Then, we had songs. After a while, I would let them choose a song. It often was the same favorite I did with actions.

I really loved the job, and Michael was with me. The building had a big open area under the house and for breaks there were tricycles, scooters, and all kinds of balls. I felt so blessed by God that I had that opportunity to do something that gave me so much joy.

TRAVELING FROM HONG KONG

Our First Furlough Since Arriving in Hong Kong

In 1966, on our first furlough since arriving in Hong Kong, we were privileged to travel to so many places. We always traveled with chartered flights to save money. We were given the amount of funds to fly from Hong Kong to St. Louis, the mission headquarters, and return. By flying cheaper, we could afford to go to Europe because I wanted to visit my family. Our first experience was that our scheduled flight out of Hong Kong had engine problems, and we waited for hours at the airport. After a while, we were assigned to a hotel in downtown Kowloon that the airline provided for us. Since we had such a big send off from all the people who had become our friends, it seemed weird to be put up in a hotel in Kowloon.

When we finally left, we stopped in several places on our way to Europe. Our first stop was in Beirut, Lebanon. We visited with a missionary family with a classmate of Manfred's. This was a beautiful university city at the time and many Europeans vacationed at its beaches. Later, war broke out and much of the city was destroyed. That was a shame.

From Beirut, we flew to Jerusalem and spent a few days sightseeing and even attended the Lutheran worship service on Sunday. It was very hot during the day, but at least it cooled down at night. The girls even got to ride on a camel. This was before Israel opened, so we did not get to see it, but we saw Bethlehem and Jericho and the Dead Sea. It seems so long ago, but walking in the old town of Jerusalem made me appreciate a little of what it must have been like in the days Jesus walked these same roads bearing the cross of Calvary. I wish I had made more of an effort to really feel what it must have been like when Jesus was on earth, but because of the

heat, and my youth, and my occupation with my very young girls, my precious daughters, I didn't get as much out of it as I wanted. We stayed at a German Lutheran hostel that served all the meals and even took care of the girls while we were sightseeing with a local guide driving to various places. I think now that Manfred got a lot more out of that tour. My only thought was that I was going to die from the heat since the only drink was small Coke bottles. Now I wish I had paid more attention.

We took a charter flight to Europe, visited my family and friends, and did sightseeing. As I came to understand, Manfred was a great planner. He planned this furlough along with the other four furloughs and did it all by mail which took tenacity in those days. He wrote to each Chamber of Commerce, the churches in which he wanted to preach, and the national parks of every place we planned to visit to get information about the area to make our trip more efficient and enjoyable. He received many return letters for the various churches he had on the schedule.

This was the first time my parents got to see their grandchildren, Margarete, at three-and- a-half, and Dorothy, at two years old. It was quite a shock to the girls at first to realize that their relatives did not speak either English or Cantonese, but only German. They learned to get along just the same. It was also the first time I had seen my siblings' children, my children's cousins. In Hamburg, Germany, we stayed with my parents. They had a vacation house about twenty miles away in the country, a town called Quickborn, and we stayed there and my parents drove to Hamburg every night and returned in the mornings. That gave us some time alone which we needed. It was hard to be guests all the time. We needed the space to have devotions and prayer time with our children. Switching between two languages was tiring and stressful by the end of the day. Manfred spoke some German, but that was only in his early childhood in Argentina. Since my whole family does not believe in God, that was another stressor for us all. We had many family get-togethers since it was also my birthday during our stay. We did, however, do some sightseeing in Germany with the new Volkswagen Squareback my dad bought for us before shipping it to New York.

Then, we took another charter flight to New York and all went smoothly. We drove the Volkswagen (VW) to New Jersey to see the Ballwegs and Bielefelds and introduced them to our girls. They loved the open area with all the trees and grass to run around. Charlie, the young baker of the Bielefelds, took them on the tractor as he mowed the huge lawn. They also ran through the forest in the back where the swing was. Marie made wonderful desserts and decorated them for the girls. Anna and George's house I had not seen before, and it was where we stayed.

Manfred had made arrangements from Hong Kong, already, to give slide shows about the work there at several churches along the way to St. Louis. He gave his first slide show of the of work in Hong Kong at the church where we were married. It was a big hit and also to be reacquainted with former friends. Several of the nurses who I worked with at the Huntington Hospital came to the church. It felt like a homecoming for me, but a little over the top for our two little girls. They learned quickly that this was a new way of life because we traveled from morning to afternoon in our new car. The luggage was in the side of the back of the Squareback with one sleeping bag next to that where Dorothy took her naps. In the back seat was another sleeping bag where Margarete took naps for the many long days of driving. There were no seatbelts in those days!

We stayed in many homes of people we did not know but were members of the churches where Manfred gave the slide shows on Saturday evenings and preached Sunday mornings as a guest preacher. One memory that I just recalled when we reached a new home to stay in, was that Margarete would say, "Hi, I'm Margarete, and this is my sister, Dorothy. How many bathrooms are there in your house?" In 1960, many bathrooms were carpeted, and that, apparently, intrigued the girls.

Manfred was very good at planning and making arrangements for things such as when we would be at his parent's house at a certain time on a certain day. As we drove up in our green Volkswagen, I saw his dad coming out the front door, knowing that when Manfred said he would be there, he would. Everyone just had to fit in with his plans.

When we got to St. Louis, we stayed in a missionary apartment near the seminary. Manfred took classes and spoke on missions in the area. We spent our Christmas with Manfred's parents in Wausau, Wisconsin, so they could visit with their new grandchildren. It was a wonderful Christmas with his parents, Ernie (the youngest of Manfred's nine siblings) and us. None of the other siblings could make it. Our girls saw their first snow. The furlough came to an end quickly.

I did some nursing (3-11) shift at St.Mary's near the seminary, and just when I had started, I realized I was pregnant again. In July, we started the hot, long drive to San Francisco to spend time with Manfred's brother,

Martin, and family before heading back to Hong Kong on another charter flight. On the way to Martin's after leaving St. Louis, we stopped at several churches for evening mission lectures. We sold the Volkswagen to Martin because he wanted it, and we were leaving to go back to Hong Kong after a yearlong furlough. Martin had that car for many years until his daughter finally wrecked it in an accident.

Returning to Hong Kong After Our First Furlough

Back in Hong Kong, I was aware again how hot and humid it was and how our apartment smelled musty, and all our belongings were covered in mold. After lots of cleaning and drying with heating lamps, we soon felt at home again. One of our daily battles were cockroaches (large ones) which scared the girls. Earlier, they never were really aware of them, and I was like a maniac trying to get rid of them. The girls always turned on the big light if they had to go to the bathroom and check their slippers and bathroom for roaches.

It was time for Margarete to start school. The British government built a brand new elementary school. It was called Beacon Hill School which was named after the place in which it was located. We applied, thinking she would go into kindergarten only to learn that children start first grade the year they turn five. That was a surprise, but she was more than ready! The principal, Mr.Cheeney, was a wonderful teacher and really brought excitement into the classroom for the children to want to learn. The school taught not only the basics, but Mr.Cheeney was an artist in his field and did musicals with all the children twice a year. Margarete was always anxious to get to school and loved it so much. I remember recording the play, *"Oliver Twist,"* and years later listening to them even when we were already in Pocatello, and it was so much fun. They had this strong British accent that it gave me goose bumps. There were such great memories from that school that I will never forget. All our children started school there. What a blessing—every morning they had prayer at that school.

Annually, the school had a fundraising event. I would spend hours sewing on my newly-purchased Bernina sewing machine. I made clothes for baby dolls and Barbie dolls, which was always a hit with the kids and parents. Materials bought in the market places were very cheap, and they had great variety. That was one of the ways I spent a lot of time. I loved sewing and made all the children's uniforms for school and dresses too. For the boys, I made shirts. I also made pajamas for the children for Christmas. For the plays, I made a lot of costumes. That was a way that I could be of help for the school plays.

Since the standard of living in Hong Kong was very high, we were so lucky that the mission paid for our housing, but, still, we often ran out of money before the next month's salary came. We often prayed and thanked God that we could trust in Him to supply our needs. Sometimes we even prayed for a specific amount, and it came from churches in the United States almost always to the amount needed. At first I seldom believed it would work like that but soon started to trust that God really heard our prayers.

During this term, we moved into one of the two houses the church owned. We moved into the upstairs apartment of #19 Oxford Road. It was wonderful. This was also good because in November we were expecting our third child. Manfred had an office in the upstairs room by the roof that was meant for servant quarters, and we actually had three bedrooms to use for sleeping, all with air conditioners, and a very large living room and separate dining room and kitchen. We felt so fortunate to have all that room.

We spent that Thanksgiving at the Winkler's, in the other mission house across the street, #32 Oxford Road. The next day, I had our son, Richard Mark. We were excited to have a son after the two girls, but my doctor said, no more children. We very quickly decided Richard needed a brother because the girls were such good company for each other, so we started the adoption process right away. Manfred wrote letters and fulfilled all the necessary requirements. He stated that we would like a boy and when he was asked for the time frame of his birth he said between April and June of 1970 would be the best when we have our next furlough. We prayed about this and knew if it was God's will it would happen, and if not, we would also be okay. We had not shared this with the girls since we didn't want to get their hopes up for nothing.

Our Travels to Europe and America and Adoption of Michael

In 1970, Richard was just over two years old. Since we would be gone from February to the end of June on this furlough, it took a lot of creative packing. We had to put all our belongings in one room at the house, so they could use our house for others while we were gone. This furlough was different because the three children and I went to Europe and Manfred to St. Louis to study for six months to complete his doctoral thesis he had been working on for a long time while in Hong Kong.

Our airplane ride took many stops in Bangkok, Thailand; Ceylon, Sri Lanka; and New Delhi, India. Here we had to change planes. Our next flight was on Swiss Air to Zurich. New Delhi had no modern toilet, and I had to hold the girls over the hole that was supposed to be for squatting. Also, the airports all had cigarette ashtrays which made it hard to keep the kids clean. Before arriving in Zurich, Switzerland, the girls ate so much chocolate on the plane that they got very sick and vomited in the car when Mr. Krause, a family friend, who had met us at the airport, drove us to his home in Southern Germany.

From the Krauses, we traveled by train up to a suburb of Hamburg and had a great time staying with my sister, Hella, at her house. She had one boy, Olaf, and a girl Margarete's age called Jutta. We saw my parents, my brothers and sisters, and did a lot of fun activities, like when my dad took us to the Hamburg zoo. But mainly, we just relaxed and enjoyed time spent with family, and I looked forward to being with Manfred again after a long separation. While at my sister's, I went to a neighborhood church on Sundays and got stared at for bringing children to church. They had a separate Children's Church but since our children didn't speak German, I wanted them in the service with me. The liturgy was the same, and our children sang it in English. People were amazed after a while by how good my three children behaved in church, but we still never felt really welcomed. It was strange and different for me because the attending church members were dismissed after service because only the "real members" of the church could stay for communion. A church member would have to register on the Saturday before to have communion the next day. It was a real conservative Lutheran Church.

At the end of March, we flew to New York and went to the Ballwegs and Bielefelds in Flemington, New Jersey, for a few days. We also visited the church where we got married and renewed some friendships.

The Ballwegs and I on one of our visits on furlough

Richard fell asleep the last half hour of our flight to America, and I had to carry him. The girls were a big help but could not lift those suitcases. Finally, I put Richard on one of the suitcases on the conveyor belt. I can't remember who picked us up, but I think it was Albert, one of the bakers in Flemington. He was the only one who had a car. George had a Jeep but would have been too nervous to drive in the city. The sad part on that furlough was that Marie had gotten Alzheimer's. She was the one who decorated all the cakes and made our wedding cake. She was always very small, but now she looked really tiny sitting in a child's high chair. Anna was taking care of her. She smiled at us but did not speak, and I don't think she knew who I was. That was the last time I saw her.

When I was ready to fly to St. Louis from Newark Airport, I was more than ready to see Manfred and have him take care of me and the children for a while. There was a "slow strike" at the airport in which the employees would slow down the time it would take them to do their jobs, and we ended up sitting in a hot plane for almost four hours. When it was ready to take off, the fuel was too low, and we had to go back to the gate, deplane, and refuel. We finally took off six hours late with three hungry, tired, crabby children. I was dead tired and had no way to contact Manfred on the other end. When we finally arrived in St. Louis, Missouri, Manfred was not at the gate and then I lost it and started to cry. Then, I saw Florence Winkler, our dear missionary friend from Hong Kong who was also on furlough. She said that Manfred was here and was just making inquiries about the flight. It was so good to see him. I didn't realize how much I missed him until I saw him again—what a sweet reunion! I thanked God for bringing us back together, and knew I never wanted to be apart again for that long a time.

Manfred was still busy with finishing his thesis, and we settled in at the apartment near the seminary. After just a couple of days, we got a phone call from the adoption agency asking us if we still wanted a baby. They had two available, one was just born, and the other was due at the end of April. They thought the later one would fit better into our family. We told them we would wait since Manfred was still busy with completing his studies. On April 21, 1970, our baby was born. We shared this with the children, and they were very excited and wanted to get him right away. We talked about names and shared we could not pick him up until June 11 (he would be my birthday present).

On June 10, 1970, Manfred had his final doctoral oral examinations. He was stressed getting ready for defending his thesis to a big examining board. He passed and received his doctorate—halleluiah!

The next day, we drove 373 miles to Milwaukee, Wisconsin, at a speed limit of fifty-five mph at the time, by leaving early and arriving at 3:00 p.m. at Elsie Hatstead's home, a distant relative of Manfred's. We cleaned up, dressed up the children, and went to pick up Michael. It was love at first sight for all of us. We had a ceremony of baptism and Margarete just stared at the baby, who was now seven weeks old. He just kept smiling at her. Because we only had one bottle of formula given to us, we decided to just go back to St. Louis, and we drove straight through, and Michael slept the whole way (a wonderful start with our completed family of six).

We had to get a passport and visa for Michael to take him to Hong Kong with all the adoption papers because the adoption would be finalized in Hong Kong. In August, we were ready to fly to San Francisco. I was packing and pulled my back so badly that I couldn't get off the floor and ended up in the emergency room. I used pain medicine and a corset, so I could travel the next day. Poor Manfred was all worried about me holding up with four children. We still didn't get the passport and visa for Michael. Martin's family took good care of us for a few days, and the passport was in the mail the day we were ready to leave. Martin and Manfred actually had to find the mailman on his route to get it in time to go to the airport.

Returning from our furlough, we had a stopover in Seoul, Korea, and arrived there in time for dinner and spent the night. Michael had slept on the whole flight over, so he was ready to play while the rest of us wanted to sleep. The next day, we went back on the plane to Hong Kong. It was nice to get home again—only we had to move all our things from the upstairs apartment to the downstairs which had been painted and fixed up for us when we returned. That is where we lived until we returned to America for good in 1977.

In 1973 we had another furlough, and it was pretty much the same as the previous ones. We went to Europe and then America spending some time with Karl-Heinz, my brother and family, and the Ballwegs and Bielefelds. At that time, we bought a big Oldsmobile station wagon in New Jersey, which served us well traveling across American with four children. My brother, Gert, and his "wife" (significant other) from Germany, were also at my brother's house to visit. In the car all together, we were singing at the top of our voices in German and laughed a lot; it was so much fun.

Another highlight of my life with my children was that about one-and-a-half miles from the house was a Dairy Queen and my children and my brother's children walked there for ice cream cones. On every trip when we drove long distances and when they saw a Dairy Queen ad sign, they would say, "Have you DQ'd today?" which was their slogan. Every day there were long stretches of travel ending around two to three in the afternoon. It was either a church where Manfred would speak or at a National Park where we stayed in cabins. Every step of the way was well-planned ahead by Manfred. We went back to St. Louis, a shorter stay this time, then we went the Northern route winding our way through Wisconsin, Minnesota, Montana, and Washington, and again, to Martin's in Palo Alto, California. We had a stop at Holden Lake in Washington for four days and that was very different and enjoyable and made us fall in love with the Northwest.

During the different flights, the children always found friends to play games with, mostly card games or drawings of *hangman* or *tic tac toe*. On the planes, they were not yet so strict with seatbelts and smoking. Smokers were seated in the back of the plane. Manfred always got sick on planes and took Dramamine and slept most of the way.

After another three-month furlough in 1976, we went back to Hong Kong. The mission work had become very frustrating because for the past few years, there were politics in the church, both in the United States and in Hong Kong. I won't go into details about that, but it clearly affected Manfred and work became frustrating and stressful. Also, our children were getting to an age where they needed to think about education in the future.

My Children's Education and Friends I Made

Our children went to a school that taught English which was excellent for them .The teaching was a different method. There was no such thing as a multiple choice question. You had to write the answers long hand. It was quite a shock at first to understand the American way for our children. They adjusted quickly, but it was very hard because of their very strong British accents. Hong Kong was a British colony at the time. Margarete and Dorothy went to the Hong Kong International School for our last year which helped them adjust to the American way of learning.

My best friend, aside from the missionary wives, was Traute. She was married to a Chinese businessman that she met in England during college. She is Austrian, and we spoke German together. Traute had three children close in age to my children. I met her at a park when the children were very young, and we became friends. The children would play and we would talk. Her family was rich and the fear that her children might become abducted was always a problem and a worry. The children were brought to school in a Rolls Royce with a chauffeur. It was clear they came from money. Traute picked them up in a Mercedes. Because I lived in a closed-in (gated) mission house, she and the children often came after school to our house.

We often talked about religion. She grew up Catholic but did not attend church. I learned how to share my love for Jesus and the church, and she asked many questions. She still talks about our friendship when I Skype with her now. God gives us so many opportunities to share his love for all people. Many times I see the chances I missed after the fact and know God understands-that gives me peace.

Alice Lee became one of my Chinese friends. It started with her wanting to learn English, but after a while, she often came because she enjoyed our family. She became a Christian and attended church regularly. She especially enjoyed Margarete, our oldest daughter, and after we left, she came to Canada and still kept her friendship with Margarete through letters and cards for birthdays after they got reacquainted through Facebook.

I made other friends as well, but they were not as close. Many were the wives of pastors who graduated from the seminary.

POCATELLO, IDAHO

Leaving Hong Kong

We made the decision, after much prayer, to leave Hong Kong in the summer of 1977. We sold or gave away everything we had except for a few items we wanted to keep as mementos for the wonderful years spent there. When we returned to America, we landed in Los Angeles. Richard, my nine-year-old, stepped out of the plane and said, "Wow, they even air condition the outside in America!" It was cool and beautiful—no humidity.

From there, we got on a train to go to San Francisco where Manfred's brother picked us up. We enjoyed time together with his family before flying to St. Louis. There we had to be checked and do the paperwork for getting out of the missionary role and be put on the pastors' list. Manfred put his name on the Northwest District Call List.

A small crate was sent off to Portland, Oregon, because we felt the urge to come to the beautiful Northwest. We had no call yet, but Manfred had found an empty parsonage for us to live in by Concordia University in Oregon. St. Michael's Church was right next door, and that's where we went to church for almost four months. Manfred preached at churches in the area, and we went to church at St. Michael's while waiting for a call to somewhere in the Northwest. We also spent a week at Holden Village again, and Manfred's youngest brother, who was a professor in Vancouver, British Columbia, at the time, joined us with his family of two boys.

Manfred received three choices, one to San Francisco, Chinatown, which he didn't feel he wanted to do at the time; one to an island by Seattle (Mercer Island); and one to Pocatello, Idaho. Just a couple of weeks before that call to Pocatello came, we were in Tillamook, Oregon, where Manfred preached, and a lady told me after church she wished we would get a call to Pocatello, where she came from, because they needed a good pastor. She said that they were a struggling congregation. I had no idea where Pocatello was and just put that thought out of my mind. When that call came, we looked it up on the map. I didn't even know where Idaho was.

In August, when we received the call to Pocatello, Manfred and I drove there to see if we were a good fit for Grace Lutheran Church on Tenth Street. Gabe and Karen, a young couple and one of them a teacher at Grace School, hosted us in their home. The church struggled because they had experienced several pastors who had stayed on for only a short time and left. We looked at housing even though there was a small parsonage next to the church. Since we had never owned a house, Manfred and I really wanted to start having a home that was more permanent and our children could call home as they grew up. That seemed to be a good sign to the church members that maybe we would stay there. Manfred accepted the call and bought a house for $46,000 that we had picked out when we had visited. We moved there in October. We spent a lot of time in prayer together that this move was the will of God.

When we drove into Pocatello with a U-Haul, Dorothy said to me, "Why are we moving here. There are no people." This was a big shock to her after Hong Kong and Portland where they had started school during the four months we were there.

It was a time of adjustment for all of us. Margarete in high school, Dorothy's last year in middle school, and the boys, Richard and Michael, in Grace Lutheran Elementary school in fifth and second grade, respectively.

It was a shock to me because I had always lived by the water in Hamburg, Germany; Staten Island, New York; Hong Kong, China; and now we were in dry Pocatello, Idaho. From my kitchen window, I could see the American Falls reservoir, the closest thing to water.

I still had my nursing license from New York which I kept up, but I wanted an Idaho license. To review, I spent a few hours at Idaho State University with tapes and books. I had to learn many new skills after ten-plus years of not working in a hospital. I had never started IVs or read EKGs, but I studied and learned quickly. I started working at the old St. Anthony's Hospital, working nights in ICU. It was a little scary because the nurse I was working with thought I had enough orientation to do all the work, and he often just slept.

At that time, there was only an LPN in the ER, so when there was "a code" the nurse from the ICU had to run down to the ER and run the code until a doctor that was "on call" came. One night I was called to the ER and worked "a code" alone. The supervisor came to relieve me from ICU, so I ran down to the ER. That was a scary experience. It seemed like the doctor never was going to come. I finally said, "When is the doctor coming?" The whole time he was already there, but I had never met or seen him before. He looked like an Indian with his haircut and ordinary clothing—not like a doctor at all.

He said, "You are doing a great job and keep it up." This was a huge learning experience and I realized that I needed to feel more confident.

As I write my stories, these memories come to me in my dreams. At the time, when I was still a nursing student, one of the drugs we used regularly for preoperative patients was Nembutal, a pretty yellow capsule to help people to sleep and be more relaxed for surgery the next day. It really worked well. The other drug was Seconal in an orange capsule, and it worked the same. Neither drug is on the market anymore because they were so dangerous and often misused causing many deaths.

Another memory is that oxygen was not built into the walls. We had the big green tanks and had to change them when they ran empty. The orderlies would do it if they were available, but we had to keep an eye on them to make sure they didn't run empty. Also, there was no suction equipment built into the walls for nasogastric (ng) tubes. It ran on a Wangensteen pump that looked a little like a big egg timer which we had to rotate to give suction. It was filled with water which was another item we had to keep your eye on.

Nursing was so very different when I came back in 1977 in Pocatello. I did work for a couple of months in St. Louis on the 3-11 shift, but the changes from 1966 to 1977 were amazing, and the changes in medicine seem to get faster and better.

Arriving at Our New House in Pocatello, Idaho

When we arrived at our "new" house that we had bought on our first visit when we accepted the call, I was shocked to see so many people standing there. These were the members of our "new" church welcoming us with open arms. Everyone was ready to meet our children and to move us in. It was a great surprise since we were tired from packing the U-Haul and driving all day. I had to quickly look inside the house again to decide where to put our belongings.

Before I knew it, all was moved in and even all the beds were made and dinner was on the table. Almost right away, I felt that yes, God, this is the place where you want us to be. Manfred rounded up all the helpers and thanked them for their help and prayed for our future there together serving God. We still had many boxes to open later, but we had time for that.

First we had to start finding out about schools for our children. It was easy for the boys because they could walk to the school that belonged to the church on Pershing Avenue. Dorothy had to go to the middle school for ninth grade which was very hard. I'm sure she was thinking that every person already had friends for the year and here comes the new student with a British accent. Nowadays, that would be cool, but not at that time. Also, most of the girls were Mormon which we knew very little about at the time. Margarete went to high school and seemed to adjust better as far as I remember. She graduated in 1980 and went to college at Concordia University in Portland.

Grace Lutheran Church on Tenth was a beautiful old church, but it had a very small parking lot. When we were still in Portland, the former principal of Grace approached Manfred and said, "Whatever you do, don't talk about a new building." He explained that the church was split by building a separate school on Pershing Avenue. After we had been there awhile, it seemed to Manfred that none of the Elders or Counsel had any plans or vision for the future.

Manfred had already made a number of calls on members and visitors to start a "Basic Bible Truth" class and some said they would attend, but very few showed up on Sundays. He was very discouraged which made me sad, but I prayed it would change. Some members thought he was hard to understand when preaching because of his accent. Since he grew up in Argentina, with his mother speaking German and Spanish at school, all the children in his family of ten had an accent. Coming to America at the age of thirteen with his family, he added American English to his language. He then decided to take a class at Idaho State University in Pocatello to improve his speech.

At one of the Elder meetings after a few months, the church telephone rang and someone answered it and said that it was for him from Switzerland. When we were still in Hong Kong, that was one of the places Manfred had applied to for a possible position after we finished there, but we never heard back from them. Now, he got the phone call from them, and he explained to them that he had accepted the call to Grace and that he was really needed and this was not the time for change. When the elders heard about this, they realized that Manfred made a commitment to this church and had no plans to leave. From that point on, everything changed. Suddenly, they felt better about the job that Manfred tried to explain to them—that calling and visiting each member was not his alone because it is for every member, especially the elders. Pretty soon, he had a large membership class. Manfred's greatest gift from God, in my opinion, was recognizing leader potential and encouraging others.

I, on the other hand, was put on the school board since they knew I ran a school in Hong Kong. That decision scared me. I barely got to know the people on the board and did not think I was qualified to make the right choices. I read all the past minutes and prayed for wisdom. Manfred was so supportive; it gave me courage. I know it says in the Bible(Philippians 4:13) that we can do all things through Christ who gives us strength. So I trusted in that verse that God would supply what I needed.

It didn't take me long to realize that the part-time principal, who also taught second grade half-day, needed to be a full time principal. We only had three or four classrooms in the building, and one was in the basement. Some grades were combined. It did not take long for the now full-time principal to change that, and the school grew.

Gabe, the principal, was a man with a vision and helped Manfred also to realize the vision he had for the future of Grace. But after the warning from the previous Grace School principal in Portland, Oregon who said that whatever you do don't bring up building because when building the separate school on Pershing Avenue the church had a split, Manfred was very cautious in bringing up what he knew needed to happen to grow the church by making members aware that everyone of them must be a disciple in this growth and, consequently, would necessitate a larger church and school.

Now, of course, I had a job at the hospital and to start it had always been a choice for evening shifts or night. I ruled evening out because then I would hardly get to see the children, so I worked nights. It was good for learning, but not for my health, because I could seldom sleep during the day. Manfred would make big signs by the stereo, TV, and by the entrance—"Mom Is Sleeping," but that did not help that much, but I loved him so much for caring about me.

In January 1978, several members from Grace went to the Marriage Encounter put on in a hotel by the Catholic Church. They returned to church with a report and excitement of what it had done for their marriages. They encouraged us to attend the next one. At first, I was not excited to go because I thought we had a very satisfying relationship. Members signed us up, and we did attend the next one. It is hard to explain, but both of us became aware how much we actually needed this. In some ways, we were living two separate lives and did not realize what we had been missing in our relationship. We were just as "giddy" about it as were the previous couples who encouraged us to go. It didn't take long for Manfred to say, "We need a Lutheran version of this." He quickly learned there was a Lutheran Marriage Encounter started in Spokane, Washington, and one in Orange County, California, and that one couple was a presenter in California and lived in Idaho Falls at the time.

This complicated my life. Trying to sleep because of nursing at night, I slept, maybe, two hours, woke up and started writing talks for Marriage Encounter. Each talk was then work-shopped by a committee or an experienced leader couple called an Administrative Couple.

Every LME presenter follows a prescribed outline. There are four couple presenters at each LME weekend. There is "a Rookie," the newest work-shopped couple, then a Mid couple, and a Lead couple (Administrative Couple) who is in charge. They have all presented before. There is one Clergy Couple, and they have to write all the thirteen talks. Two couples present at a time, a Clergy and a Rookie, or a Mid, or a Lead. The talks build on each other and really make you think, not just about yourself, but ending with your relationship to God and the church. "I'll Never Find Another You" by the Seekers (*see internet for the words*) was our theme song. The weekends were not easy and often very trying. Many a Friday night, sitting in front of expecting couples who probably got talked into going on a weekend like we were, I was so tired after a hard work week.

Couples are not told much about the weekends. If some of them, especially the men, would have known they had to write so much and work on relational stuff, they would not have come. Usually after Friday talks, they get a glimpse of what was ahead. Seldom did we ever have couples who left the weekends, but I'm sure they thought about it. The weekends are always free of charge, but there is a talk on Sunday mornings for couples to help us make the dream, "I'll Never Find Another You," a reality.

Most couples are very generous, but some are not financially able to give. They put a note in the provided envelope, and it is very touching to read them at our meetings after the weekend is over. All the notes are heartfelt, and I'm thankful that finances are not what matters .It is all about the commandment, "Love one another as I (Christ) loved you."

There is a communion service that ends the official weekend. All weekends end with a "send off" when the couples from previous weekends (prayer couples) joined us along with the involved couples' children, including ours. The children realized what an exciting experience this was. It was very infectious. It seemed like we had been on a long, long journey even though it was just Friday evening to Sunday afternoon. I was thrilled to see my children and share our experience.

We presented our first Lutheran Marriage Encounter weekend in November 1978 in Pocatello, which was the first for our Rookie couple as well. They were members of Grace Lutheran Church in Pocatello. Two couples had the experience already in California. The best part of LME was that it was a ministry that Manfred and I did together. We ended up presenting ninety-eight weekends from 1978 to 2010.

I am very aware that it brought many couples to be much closer to God and each other. Many couples became presenters and so enjoyed serving God in his ministry. On the other hand, it also made some couples aware of the fact that they did not seem to be right for each other. That was also hard, but it gave them better understanding why they were not happy. Manfred, being the pastor, and me by his side, led to many opportunities in the evening to help couples who had many questions. We also served on the board for our area which included all the Northwest of America and Alaska. We even gave weekends twice in Alaska. All weekends are in hotels, and after presentations, couples were given a question to write on for ten minutes. One of the couples wrote in the conference room while the spouse went to their room to write, alternating after each presentation. Then, they had time together in their rooms until they were called to the next session or lunch, etc. It was a very powerful, emotional weekend every time.

At first, we had as many as thirty couples and trying to get to know them during the weekend really stretched my brain. Every weekend had its own flavor depending on the people in the room. We were thankful to God for allowing us to be able to be in this ministry and that the church was so supportive and allowed us the time to go. I used to think that after the first couple of weekends there was nothing left for us to share, but it was never a problem.

So that a weekend would not just be a one-time experience, there was what we called "10 and 10's." We were given a list of questions to start at home. We were encouraged to choose the best time of the day to share what we had written. Ten minutes to write, then exchange our papers and read what the partner wrote, and share that for ten minutes. Manfred and I continued this habit for almost all the years together. Sometimes we did not have time and that was alright, but it helped us stay close to each other and to God. In retirement, this was our morning time together as we did our devotions, prayers, and "10 and 10's." We used the "Chicken Soup" books for ideas for new questions to dialogue. Also, Alice Gray's book called, *Stories for the Heart,* was very good and really helped us to search for our love for each other and for God's love for us, which is unconditional.

Grace Lutheran Church and School, Pocatello, Idaho

Grace Lutheran Church and School
The fulfillment of a dream!

One of the highlights of my life has been the people God has surrounded me with---who helped me become who I am today. I have followed in Your footsteps, Jesus, because my love for you has grown and is still growing.

Some of my best years have been the twenty-three years in Pocatello. Not only because of my great experiences with nursing and all the friends I made working at the hospital, but also my years spent with the people at Grace. Those years were exciting because we followed a dream to bring more people to know God and experience His love.

We started out in the old church on Tenth Avenue in Pocatello, and I did not even think about it not being enough. We had very nice families, but soon Manfred talked about the small parking lot and the danger of people parking on the streets. It was a concern with the children crossing busy roads to get to church as we were growing in membership. We prayed about this, asking God to help us.

This is a long introduction to the whole dream and outcome of the now beautiful Grace Lutheran Church and School that is now serving God through the many dedicated workers there. Thinking back on those years, I remember how scary it was to really trust God to fulfill the big dream Manfred and Gabe Flicker presented to the congregation. I recall Manfred taking Gabe and a few leaders of the congregation to show them the lot he had found on Baldy Avenue. It seemed huge and was close to the I-15 interstate highway located on a hill of sagebrush and rocks. We were all amazed by the size of the lot and how big that dream was getting. Many did not think we could fulfill that dream and had serious doubts because some people thought they would not be able to get up that hill in the winter and feared we would lose many members. Others thought we should just stay in the area and purchase some of the old houses. The final vote was a positive one because they chose the hilly property on Baldy despite their fears .That was a blessing and a relief. It really was not a dream so much as it was the belief that through Jesus Christ we can do all things. I also remember Manfred had a dedication on a Sunday collecting some rocks and building an altar to God and asking His blessings for the construction of the church.

Many hours and days were spent with the planning and getting people to pray and become a major part of the dream. There were difficult but fun challenges along the way. The belief became so strong within the congregation that this church needed to be built that many of them lent their talents and time to help with the construction. We had professional people come in for the big part, but it would have taken years longer without all of our dedicated members and other people of the neighborhood.

Looking through the many pictures Manfred took as the construction continued shows how many of our members were working side by side. I even learned how to tape walls. When the building was almost done, I purchased tile for the school's bathrooms at a wholesale house in Salt Lake City and had a team put together to help me do the tiling in the boy's and girl's bathrooms, including the showers. It took many evenings, and sometimes I worked all day, doing the grout. Working together with others helped me to get to know many members better and it hardly seemed like work. After several years of hard work with all aspects of this big undertaking, I could just feel it was now the dream of everyone in our growing congregation.

One of the members donated an organ which was electric, but it also had some pipes. It was so beautiful to see everything come together. It was awe inspiring! A lot of work was still ahead. Ultimately, to make it all happen, we had to hire a company to raise the needed funds. Our theme song throughout this whole time of construction was "Great is Thy Faithfulness."((b) see add. info.)

By 1987, we had our first service at the new church and school. It was exciting as people carried the communion ware and the cross while we marched up to the new church— our new home for worshiping and praising God. We were not totally done and kept continuing to build. The landscaping and laying in the lawns required a lot of people and included the children from the school.

The first service of the church and school 1987

During our thirteen years still serving at grace, we kept growing and added rooms as needed. The whole undertaking was truly and richly blessed by God.

Now, when I go to visit in Pocatello and go to church services there, I'm always filled with joy to see how much more continues to be added and how the church membership is growing and growing. Grace now has a whole new building for the high school and even an events center rented to the city for much needed space for gymnasiums for volleyball, racket ball, invitational games, and other activities. There is also a new area for private meetings for psychological and counseling support.

The biggest blessing is Pastor Jonathan Dinger who also has a vision for how to bring Christianity to this very Mormon community through constant outreach in the area. Now they even have two wonderful pastors.

There is so much to be thankful for, and my heart overflows with joy, thinking how much of a blessing that ministry is in Pocatello and surrounding areas in the form of Grace Lutheran Church and School. All of this is a great gift from God to this small area of southeastern Idaho. God is smiling down when He sees the people and hard work there. We all honor Him through this school and house of worship. And the work and dedication continues even today. It is an awesome place to worship and to love one another as Jesus commands us to do.

Youth Group at Grace Lutheran Church

In 1983, we had a young DCE (Director of Christian Education) who had a youth group for high school teenagers but not middle school children. I wanted Michael to start going to youth group, but no one volunteered to start it, so I did. I recruited seven other parents to help me get started. I made personal visits to all the kids in that age group at their homes to meet the parents and find out who was willing to support it. We were still at the old church at the time, so I decided to have it in our house. To my surprise, or should I say shock, I had almost forty boys and girls. All my helpers took various jobs to support this group. There was one for snack, some for games and activities, and several helped with devotions, Bible study, and singing. It was not the job I thought I was gifted for, but God helped to make this a big success.

We actually were able to have many outings on weekends. One time we went rafting with overnight tenting on the banks of the Snake River. That was a big success. We also went tubing on the Portneuf River by Lava Hot Springs. Another activity was a bike trip. The hardest for us was the overnighters at the old school, and later, at the new church and school. We had to keep a close eye on the boy/girl friends. The overnighters called "lock-ins" had strict rules, but, of course, rules are made to be broken by teenagers. The mornings ended with a big breakfast. To entertain during the night, we rented a VCR (videocassette recorder) at the store and some movies. The favorite was the Karate Kid. No one then had VCRs at home.

Since I started Junior Youth Group, I was so blessed with all the people who volunteered their time. There are so many great stories how God blessed this ministry. Even in a church setting, there are many children in that age group who feel unsure of themselves or even misunderstood and very insecure. Spending weekly time with the group, you get to recognize which children need extra attention and love. When we organized Thanksgiving dinners for the elderly one year, I asked this girl who I knew was really struggling if she would bake a pie because she volunteered to help. Her mom wrote in a letter that when she brought the pie, I gave her a "bigggggggg" hug and encouraged her. She also wrote that "she can remember her (daughter's) smile, the smile we hardly ever saw at that time in her life." Of course, I don't really remember that incident, but it gives me joy even now as I write it.

There are so many wonderful events during those years because we had so many opportunities to love and pray with those kids. They enjoyed the Bible studies, but even more the planned activities. Since we had several volunteers, different children connected with different adults which was so great.

One girl in particular—I won't say more about her—-gave me a bunch of grey/white hairs for sure. She always disrupted the group when we tried to learn more about the endless love Jesus has for us. She spent some time on the bench on my deck. I praise God because she is now a wonderful parent.

One thing I was never aware of before was that if one girl had to go to the bathroom, three or four had to go with her. The boys used to make fun of that.

I think I learned a lot in those years about teenagers and patience. Looking back at that time, and remembering the people I worked with, brings back the good old days and the fun we had.

Grace Youth Group rafting the Snake River 1989

Throughout my ten years of working with the youth groups, all my helpers were faithful and were outstanding in their commitment to the kids. Soon, the church hired a full-time DCE for both youth groups since the church had so many new members *((c)see add.info.)*

The Senior Youth Group Director

Marty Meyer

The Missouri Synod Lutheran Church is well-known for its many schools. Some are high schools, quite a few colleges, and two seminaries. They specialize in training teachers, DCE's (Director of Christian Education), Deacons, and Deaconesses. The seminary training comes after college degrees. It's a four-year training for pastors that serve our many churches and missionaries all over the world. During the third year, the young (some older after a secular job also) are assigned to one of the churches, to work with the pastors of that church where they will work. It is very intensive training for them. In school, they are fairly sheltered and surrounded by all Christian servants of God.

This year away is called a vicarage. Manfred was assigned to Trinity Lutheran Church in Queens, New York. After his fourth year back in seminary in St. Louis, he made the decision to stay another year for his Masters in Divinity. The summer after he finished, he wanted to do another vicarage in the New York area, called the Atlantic District, which included Connecticut and New Jersey. His goal was to study areas where new churches might be planted and to help these new churches get new members. So, he traveled several places, mostly staying for two weeks at each location. That was how God planned for us to get to know each other, and as I have already shared, in Flemington, New Jersey.

This is sort of an explanation why I had met this young man, Marty Meyer, in Pocatello. The church hired him as a DCE, especially for youth work. His family was all working in Christian education. Marty's father, Bob, was a professor at St. John's College in Winfield, Kansas. His mom, Milly, was an art teacher. He was wonderful and spirited for the young people at Grace. He also led the youth group after I was finished with it.

After he came, he was just a lonely, single man. I started doing a Tuesday night dinner at our house to get to know him better and help him to get to know our young teachers and single people. It became sort of a highlight in my life and in his also.

He ended up getting married at Zion Lutheran Church in Nampa, Idaho, after a lengthy courtship with a beautiful, young lady named Kelly who was finishing her teaching degree at Idaho State University. It was a beautiful wedding like most I have seen because, to me, all weddings are beautiful because it is a happy time with young people in love.

I learned a lot about his family because they had been part of Camp Perkins for many years already. In fact, my son Richard really got to know Carrie at Camp Perkins. Carrie is now my daughter-in-law, and she and Richard are parents of four of my grandchildren.

Marty felt the calling from God to be a missionary and left our church to follow his calling. I am very proud of this wonderful couple and keep them in my prayers often. They started the "Youth with a Mission" in Cascade, Idaho, and have been many places in the world to bring God's love to the needy. They are a blessing to God. Marty has written two books about his mission work. God is really blessing his life's work and uses him mightily. Thank you God for letting me witness how you can work in people's hearts.

Grace Youth Group mission to Mexico

Back to Nursing

After updating my skills in nursing and working to get an Idaho license, I worked at the old St. Anthony's Hospital. It didn't take too long before there was an opening in the intensive care unit, and critical care unit, that was offered to me. Much like building a new church, they were also building a new hospital up on another hill on North Center Street. It was called Pocatello Regional Medical Center and was very beautiful. The other hospital in town was Bannock Hospital.

I loved being back in nursing and was the first one who took a patient to the new Intensive Care Unit. I had a tour of the facility, but thought I would get lost with all the rooms and offices I could not remember. Working in the units was my favorite. I loved giving full-care for my patients, but I also got acquainted with all the different floors. To me, that was important. If the units were not full, I could work other areas. It helped me to get to know so many more nurses and personnel. I loved what I was doing and Manfred often said, "She would do it even if they didn't pay her." That is probably an overstatement.

One time while working on the medical floor, I was assigned several patients. There was one old lady who gave everyone a hard time, and she was assigned to me. Her room was right across from the nurses' station. After caring for her and introducing myself by name, she seemed to be no problem at all. She came to Idaho, as she got older, to be with family. She came from Brooklyn, New York, so we had much in common. While caring for another patient down the hall, I heard a loud call. She was yelling for me and calling me "Texas," and everybody was laughing. It took me a moment to realize she was calling me by associating my name with a state-Utah!

Since I have always been known for being efficient, and organized, and taking good care of my patients, I was also assigned to some of the sickest patients which was hard, but I loved the challenges. Working in CCU, the cardiac unit forced me to really learn the importance of understanding heart sounds and reading the EKGs. Since the physician only sees patients for a few minutes a day, they relied heavily on the nurse's notes and laboratory reports. Often they said they really could not work without good nurses. That encouraged all of us to do our best.

Many of the patients were grateful for our care, but there were always a few that gave us a hard time. One morning after report from the night shift, the nurse shared that the young man in his forties had a heart attack but refused her care. She was totally frustrated. He was to be my patient, so I went into the room and introduced myself.

"I'm your nurse today, and I hear you are being hard on the caregivers. We are here to help you, and if you don't cooperate, you need to sign yourself out."

After that, he became like a lamb. He had several thousand dollars which he wanted to keep at his bedside. I said to him that he can't have the money in his room and then I called the business office to come and put the money in the safe. He said he didn't want his wife to know he had that money. Then, he asked me to check the stock market. I explained to him that it was probably why he had a heart attack at an early age because money had become his God. He just stared at me for a while and finally said, "I think you are right." He was very cooperative from that moment on. After that incident, my nickname became "Sergeant."

There were many times when I had to be a patient advocate and challenge a doctor. Doctors appreciated when I spoke up for something that I saw had made a difference in the patient's care. After some time, I often had to fill in as supervisor. I was making rounds in the unit when I got paged from the emergency room. The cardiologist was sitting there charting. When I called the E.R., they said this doctor was screaming and being obnoxious—it happened to be the other cardiologist's partner.

I said, "I'll be right down and put him over my knee since his mother failed to do it!" Everyone laughed as they repeated what I said and Dr. C. said, "I want to come watch."

By the time I got to the ER, all was well, and he was calm and smiled at me.

I said to myself, "I wondered what ever happened to that shy, fearful, young girl? It must be the white hair!"

The arrival of our first AIDS patient was another scary time for all nurses. Not knowing about this new disease, we were all having to put them in an isolation room with the nurses wearing gowns, gloves, and masks to take care of them. It was hard on the patient because of the pneumonia. They feelings of loneliness and being scared— as scared as the nurses who cared for them.

There are any stories that every nurse could share but many you don't want to think about again. It is never easy when you become aware that you really can't fix their problems but can only try to make them more comfortable.

Working one night in CCU, one of my patients suddenly arrested. I saw it on the monitor. I called a code, and the team all showed up. She was successfully saved. She shared with me how scared she was. She was a devout Catholic and feared that she had not been good enough to go to heaven. That surprised me and really made me think. I tried to comfort her by saying, if you love Jesus, that's all you need. She was not convinced that was enough. It really started me to ask questions, and I wondered if I took it for granted that it was really enough. Now, I would have been better in really answering her, but she arrested twice more and didn't make it. I felt like a failure.

To keep on working in the units, we all had to keep on taking courses. Once I got to go to a Critical Care Conference in New Orleans.

Over 300 nurses were there sharing troubles and joys in their experiences. Most came from large teaching hospitals. Learning about what is new and changing in the monitoring equipment was both scary and exciting. People in the big units were a few years ahead of us from out West and the smaller hospitals, but we were catching up pretty fast. Nursing and medicine in general is a fast changing profession. More and more of it started to be on computers. The equipment became more technical and often the actual patient in bed attached to the equipment was hardly noticed. The monitors were watched instead. It made me realize how easy that can happen and made me feel sad.

All those years, I was a nurse we had eight-hour shifts, but slowly more and more hospitals went to the twelve-hour shifts. We followed the trend in the late 1980s. I did not like it. It was always great when you had a very sick patient, and after eight hours someone else took over. I did not want or like the change, but it happened. We went to 6 a.m. or 6 p.m. shifts (twelve long hours).

I realized that with those hours, it was nearly impossible to be able to do the things I loved. It was too late for choir practice, for youth group, for Lutheran Women's Missionary League (LWML) *((d) see add. info.)* and all the things I loved to be a part of at church. Talking with the Director of Nursing, I shared my concern. She challenged me to start something new that she thought was perfect for me. I have always been very good at starting IVs, and that news traveled throughout the hospital. She wanted me to start an IV (intravenous) Therapy Unit. The hospital paid for me to go to Salt Lake City to learn to put in central lines and start the training there because all the Intermountain Medical Centers had home and hospital IV units, and our hospital was part of that organization.

The nurse who was training me showed me all we had to do just to set up for the procedure. It was as if we were getting ready for surgery. Aware that the tip of the catheter ends up in the heart made me realize how important sterile technique was. She had notified the two hospitals in Ogden and Provo that if they had patients who needed PICC (peripherally inserted central catheter) lines placed, that they were to let us know, so that I could see other nurses perform the procedure. We were at the Salt Lake City Hospital. I was also introduced to the Home IV Central Pharmacy that would supply me with all I needed in Pocatello. I watched several lines being put in by others but was not certified until I had put three lines in under supervision. I was nervous at first as I had to explain the procedure to the patient, but it eased as I started to set up and get ready. Each time, it became easier, and I felt more comfortable.

Setting up a unit by myself was also scary. They did supply me with a cart that had all that you needed since the procedure is mostly done in the patient's room. Soon, I was putting in lines at all hours and even got called at night. I had a beeper, and the first cell phone that looked like the size of one square-shaped rye bread in the grocery store. It did not hold battery power very long but was enough for me to call in when I was paged.

Soon I had several patients at home for intravenous nourishment until they were able to eat again. The food called TPN (total peripheral nutrition) came from the pharmacy in Salt Lake City, and I had to set it up to run with a pump. A lot of patient and family education was involved. Also, Primary Children's Hospital was asking me to follow up on the children in our area of Pocatello after they left the hospital to go home. I did the dressing changes on my patients with the lines because I did not want to have any infections. As the doctors became more comfortable and aware what Hospital Home IV could do, I was overwhelmed by the expectations. I was often getting called in the middle of the night with problems by home patients or to put in lines when no one could get an IV into a very sick patient. I had nightmares, sometimes, that I had totally forgotten about a patient. Blood transfusions, platelets, chemo treatments, antibiotics, or just fluids would keep me hopping.

Before 1999, I had to hire a nurse to help me. She got certified and became not just efficient, but she also did the computer work which was new, and I really didn't even like that part of the new thing in medicine and everywhere else. I'd rather take care of patients, but I needed someone to help with paperwork for charging for the services we were doing. I had already trained another nurse to cover me when I had days off, but she did not put in lines. She did do the dressing changes and ran IVs on weekends. I also had a secretary who came from Hong Kong. She also helped me keep up with my Cantonese.

Later in 1999, on a weekend, I was ready to go for my normal daily, evening walk after dinner, and I hardly got started and my legs felt so weird; I could not go on. On Mondays I always took off, and that was my day to spend with Manfred—our date night. It was not the best day because so many restaurants were closed on that day of the week. I tried not to think about my problem with the legs but rested the rest of the weekend thinking I was overtired. Then, at work the next day, we had a Health Fair, and I was drawing blood samples. All of a sudden, I was really dizzy and left and started walking down the hall to go to the ER, but I never made it; I passed out in the hallway. Suddenly, I was a patient in the hospital. I was diagnosed with "hemolytic anemia" which the doctor thought was caused by a virus. One doctor told Manfred and me that my blood count was so low because my body was destroying itself. I thought of the game "Packman." The packman was snapping up my blood. He recommended that I should go home and get my life in order because there was no cure. I was shocked for a moment and then called my doctor, the one I worked with whose patient had MS (multiple sclerosis) and told him what they said. He was off that week, but he came to see me right away. He wanted to send me to the hospital in Salt Lake City, but I said I'd rather stay here. He then consulted with specialists in Salt Lake and started treatment with steroids and gamma globulin IVs for six days. After that, I had several blood transfusions. My partner, Debbie, had put a PICC line in my arm, but I was not aware of it.

Manfred had a service of healing after the original diagnosis. Sitting in a wheelchair surrounded by so many friends as they laid hands on me was an amazing feeling. That's when I started to cry and sob because I felt so loved. After several months, I was slowly getting off the steroid and was back at work. I remember that at first I thought that I would never get to see my grandchild who was due the next month, and now Joshua is twenty-one years old. God answered all the prayers, and I am healthier now that I have no more stress. I believe that it was the stress that caused the disease. Since I had Debbie, we shared the stress, and I volunteered a bit less at church.

In the spring of 1999, Manfred shared that he was going to retire. Our church had grown so much, and he was aware that we needed to think about the future. Right along, he had trained a Lay Minister to help him in several areas. He started a program a few years before called "Stephen's Ministry," which was a big help to take the pressure off him because others were able to help the many people who had problems.

Manfred was burned out. He wasn't sleeping at night and had to keep pushing himself. He always had a weekly small group of three or four wonderful men who he trusted and shared with. They became aware of his problem, and they arranged for him to take a full week at one of their cabins in Island Park to just relax and go fishing and do whatever he felt would help him. I was glad they stepped up, and he felt they could handle everything at church without him.

It was a stressful time, but Manfred understood also why I had suggested he retire because he saw how that amount of stress also affected the family and me. He came back and was clearer than before and felt he had to prepare the church for the change to come. He could not go and visit every new member because he had as many as twenty to thirty new members twice a year. We had a full church for two services on Sundays. Then, there were midweek services Wednesdays, and on Lent and Advent there were meetings. Every daily morning, he had devotions with the school staff and teachers, and he loved it all and worked too hard. Stephen's Ministry took quite a bit of pressure off, and I saw that as one opportunity to be able to help in that and started that training. I retired from PRMC Home and Hospital IV Therapy in June of 2000.

Stephen's Ministry is a training course to help provide one-on-one Christ centered intervention for helping hurting people started by the Lutheran Churches. The training course is intensive and based on giving love to other people. Those are people who may struggle with cancer, loss of a loved one, divorce, and depression. We are not trained counselors but mainly do a lot of listening.

With the help of the pastor, you get matched with a needing person. You try to schedule weekly meetings and usually spend an hour together.

No one else knows who we are meeting with, but in weekly meetings as a group, people ask for some help to make sure we stay on the goal and to not give advice—only listen. Over several years, I had different women care receivers that I met with and soon learned the real importance of being a good listener and learning how to start with open ended questions that would make them share. It was not always easy because I do love to talk. *((e) see add. info.)*

One of the other things started at church was that the elders and some volunteers would stop by to talk with visitors in their home the day after they visited at church. Once when I was only in my fifties, I walked up the driveway at one home, and a little boy saw me and ran inside and called, "Mom, there is an old lady coming up the driveway!" I just smiled, but the lady apologized.

Some of My Memories Related to Lutheran Marriage Encounter (LME)

Besides the many weekends that we presented in Pocatello, Lutheran Marriage Encounter also gave us the joy of getting to know many other couples around the world. There were Northwest Conferences every two years and international ones every three years. Even with me working part-time and Manfred the only pastor in a large growing church, we were blessed to be able to attend many of these. There were many well-known guest speakers at all of them.

Our first experience was a convention in St. Olaf University in Minnesota. Manfred and I flew there. I was nervous thinking I would not know anyone. I'm good at meeting people one-on-one, but never did like big crowds. Arriving at the airport and walking into the big hall was amazing because several LME couples were standing there with big signs with our names written on them. We were well-taken care of. Because we were there for a meeting before the conference, we had time to get to know some awesome couples who also were presenters.

Driving into the campus at St. Olaf's, I noticed the place was packed with people. I couldn't help but be surprised and overjoyed when suddenly I spied the three couples from Pocatello in the crowd. My heart jumped for joy, and I couldn't wait to get out of the car to go hug them. The three couples drove all the way in one car together to surprise us. We had no idea they were coming. The whole convention was so wonderful and the "warm fuzzies" they gave me then, I can feel now, in recalling that weekend. Manfred shared our experience at the next elders' meeting and also at church. Many of our members later attended weekends. The leadership understood how this program brought many couples so much joy and peace, and that is why they saw the value of giving Manfred the time to be a part of this ministry.

Traveling Weekends

Many of our weekends included traveling. We were blessed to take a trip to Finland for a World Wide Weekend Convention. To make the long trip just for four days, I said to Manfred that it was too much for me. Since travel to conventions was what we had to pay for, I felt it would not be a smart idea, so because we wanted to attend the convention and had to spend the money anyway, we decided to take an extended vacation.

I have always wanted to take a trip on a boat from Far North in Norway, so I asked him if we could, maybe, do that before the convention (have a real vacation since this was in 2006, and we were already retired). As we dialogued on this idea of an extended trip, Manfred realized what a great opportunity it was for us to see more of Europe—not just Germany, which we would also add onto the trip at the end to see family.

Our cheapest way to do our extended trip was to drive and visit Margarete my daughter, and Harold, my son-in-law, and their children in Shelton, Washington, first. We flew to Amsterdam on the first leg layover and from there to Hamburg and visited family. We drove with Hella and Rudolf to Lake Como in Italy where they have a second home. Spending time in this beautiful place high up over the lake was an amazing site and view. There were twenty-three to twenty-six switchbacks just to get to their home which is hanging down on the mountain side (three stories high). The kitchen and living room were on the top floor and already quite a few steps down from the street. In the middle are the two bedrooms and a bathroom. On the bottom was a family room with a kitchenette and another bathroom.

The house was in a little old village surrounded by many other villages all many centuries old. They had remodeled the home over the many years since they purchased it. They even had a large swimming pool heated with solar energy. To go shopping was a half-a-day trip, so you'd better make a good list, so you won't forget anything. They had a small vineyard also. It was hard work for them to keep it all up, but they enjoyed it. On the lake (besides ferries) are many sailboats and a sailing club. On weekends, you see so many sails because there is a sailing school. From high up it is quite a beautiful site. We mostly ate outside on the bottom patio in front of the family room.

Everyday we took long hikes. There were many beautiful old villages that used to be homes once upon a time. There were old fruit trees and many chestnut trees. It was a place for me to really relax (no phone, no TV). There was Wi-Fi which surprised me. We did help with some of the yard work but mostly just relaxed and played board games in the evening. After ten wonderful days, we drove back to Hamburg and the big city life.

On June twenty-ninth, we flew to Oslo, Norway, and then way up north to Kirkenes by the North Pole and the ice cap. There we got on the boat (the Hurtigruten Cruise Line) and came down the west coast all the way down to Bergen, Norway. One night we stopped and went to a midnight concert in Tromsø. All the fjords were so colorful and beautiful. As we got off the bus, I saw the sun setting on the horizon, and as I was watching it, it came right back up. That was quite a site. We stopped in many harbors on the way down because the ship was not just a tourist ship, but also a freighter and ferry. It delivered and picked up freight for usually an hour or two, and then took on passengers. We walked around the town and also saw many churches.

The tour guide in one church explained why the many churches were so ornate and decorated unlike Lutheran Churches in Europe or the United States. One of the reformation kings many decades ago (1536) was a Lutheran, and all the people were expected to be of the same faith, and those churches used to be Catholic Churches. I was surprised and amazed at that.

I was very happy we got to do that trip. The accommodations were not great but very adequate. We loved our time there and were ready for the next adventure in Finland. We spent one full day in beautiful Bergen, then flew to Helsinki, the capital, and from there to Jyväskylä. A young couple with two boys picked us up at the airport. My suitcase was not there. We spent a few days with this couple. The man was a high school teacher, and the two teenage boys also had to go to school. I soon learned almost every household had a sauna, and they also had a small pool to cool off in after sitting in the sauna. This couple also had another sauna at a lake where we went for a day after the International Lutheran Marriage Encounter Conference on the weekend. My suitcase, which had flown to Lisbon, Portugal, finally came on the day we were leaving for Hamburg, Germany. For five or six days I washed clothes at night and hung them in the sauna to dry. No one wears anything in the sauna, and at the convention after I was in the sauna, I had to run naked to jump in the lake. I wasn't alone and everyone did it, but it took some time getting used to.

The speakers at the conference had long names, but luckily everyone spoke English. It was fun to meet with couples from almost everywhere in the world. Mostly they were couples who presented— even from Australia and New Zealand. It was a great get-together, but I was pretty self-conscious wearing the same outfit every day. It was a joy to be with dedicated Christian brothers and sisters with almost all of them coming from various Lutheran Churches. I have such great memories of that visit. I just felt God's blessings surround me, and I thank him for his creation— so much variety everywhere.

From there we flew to Hamburg and spent a couple of days with my sisters and families in the Hamburg area. We flew back to Seattle, spend two days with Margarete's family, and then drove to Hailey, Idaho, which was where we lived at the time.

There were many other very impressionable weekends. The most fun were when we did the weekends in Idaho, and they had many couples we knew already from Lutheran Women's Missionary League, where I was vice-president for the Utah-Idaho area for three years, while I was still in Pocatello. One very memorable one was in Boise. It was a full weekend, and we had a clergy couple from one of the Lutheran Churches in the area. He was a pastor but was very difficult, and critical, and often was outside smoking when he was supposed to be writing, but he stayed because his wife insisted. One of our couples from Pocatello had the pastor's brother and wife on the same weekend. That brother was not a church goer, but his wife was faithful, and on Sunday morning he asked to be baptized during the Communion service at the end of the weekend. Manfred shared it with our friend couple from Pocatello and invited them to join the service since they were their prayer couple. When Manfred announced that event, the uncooperative pastor was so amazed, he broke up and cried because he knew the man never went to church even though his wife attended regularly. The uncooperative pastor said he wanted to come back on the next weekend and really experience it. It was the kind of affirmation that made it so easy for us to continue in this ministry.

More Vacations

Our life was not just work and Marriage Encounter. One of our cars in Pocatello was a Volkswagen Camper Van which Manfred drove regularly, but we also went on camping trips with the family in it. We had a couple of tents for the children. One of our first ones was the first summer in our area. We explored the Tetons and the Yellowstone areas. We went to the Forest Service presentations which were very educational and walking back to our campsite. We would sing together and many people near us would join in. The kids had a lot of fun and also told jokes. We played many card games in the light of the gas lantern. Outdoor cooking together is fun, and everything seems to taste better. I was always so happy that our four children enjoyed each other. We also explored the northern part of beautiful Idaho, so different from the southern part, with huge forests and beautiful shimmering lakes. The McCall area was also beautiful, although very touristy.

The Lutheran Churches in Southern Idaho own the camp in the Sawtooth Valley called Camp Perkins. It held summer camps for the children every summer. Our children started to attend them with others in their age group from church starting in 1978. I took them up and fell in love with the whole area, and in time, explored many of the lakes and hikes. Manfred would come up with me when we picked the children up on Friday afternoons. Sometimes we drove up on Thursdays and camped overnight on one of the campgrounds going up. From Pocatello it was at least a four-and-a-half hour drive, so it was fun to break it up and have a date.

Another Visit to Germany

In 1984, from July first through August eighth, we went to Germany again. This time was for several reasons. We drove to Denver and stayed with dear friends for a couple of days, then flew to Frankfurt. There we rented a nine-seater Volkswagen Van and bought Euros.

Manfred was quite nervous driving at first because he didn't know the car, and we were right on the autobahn with no speed limit and a lot of impatient German drivers. He got used to it pretty soon. We had all four children with us. We brought camping gear from home, including two tents. We visited friends we knew from Hong Kong for a day in Wiesbaden. Our children had been in school together. Then, we drove to visit our friends by Weil am Rhein, South Germany, and stayed there a few days. The girls both seemed to need the sleep. The rest of us walked along the Rhein River area. We saw swans and went in a gondola along a canal—very romantic and beautiful. The next day the girls picked strawberries with Gisela and then we all did a wine tour. Our next stop was Freiburg where we saw the Cathedral named for the city Freiburger Münster Kathedrale and had afternoon coffee and lunch with Manfred's aunt (his mother's sister) Tante Susel. She was happy to see us. We went up to the castle on a cable car. Then, we visited my friend from nursing school who lived with her family in Villingen. Then, we were off again to Bern and Interlaken in Switzerland. We camped in Lauterbrunnen at the Jungfrau summit camp to view the three highest and most famous mountains (Jungfrau, Mönch, and Eiger). They were majestic! There were three waterfalls coming down from the mountains Manfred got sick from driving through all the curvy roads and pretty much slept the rest of the day in the tent. Margarete and

I went swimming in the pool and the other three children went shopping. We had our first meal camping.

Our next stop was Munich. Manfred felt better after eating, a short walk, and a beer. Every day we thanked God for safety because of driving through narrow winding roads and going through dark tunnels, and I thanked him also that we all got along so well. Michael usually slept in the middle car seat because the tent got crowded with three. In Munich, we went to Dachau, the largest of several concentration camps. We were all impressed and shocked at the exhibit. There was a film about the gas chambers and the over 309 barracks. How Hitler could have had so much power to do what he did amazes me. We also saw the Olympic Village. By the campground the boys were fascinated by the topless ladies at the beach by the lake and also by the river on the way to the famous Deutsches Museum. The boys could not concentrate on the museum.

One of the reasons for the timing of this trip was that we had tickets for the famous "Passion Play" in Oberammergau. After visiting the castle called "Neuschwanstein," and taking pictures, we drove to Oberammergau. The passion plays of Christ Jesus are performed every ten years on an open stage. The stadium holds 500 people and has a huge orchestra. We were very happy our seats were right in the front of the orchestra. It lasts for five hours with one intermission. It just doesn't seem that long as it is so dramatic. Our children were mesmerized by the whole performance. God added an extra surprise to it. When Jesus said, "It is finished" a natural thunderstorm just added to the drama—an awe inspiring performance. In that year (1984), it was a special performance for Martin Luther's 400-year anniversary. At the intermission, Richard went down to the orchestra; he learned some of the instruments, and those musicians were mostly from the area and volunteered their time. Since it is usually performed every ten years, many of them were older but also many were young. Not only was Richard mesmerized by this extraordinary experience, all of us were so thankful for this opportunity and felt God's presence with us.

The beautiful castle, Neuschwanstein, on our Europe trip 1984

The two most famous castles in Germany are Hohenschwangau and Neuschwanstein, and we could see them from the distance as we drove through a part of Austria and back into Germany. After parking, the children took a bus up to the castle. Manfred and I took the opportunity to walk up. There were a lot of tourists but all were very organized as we were guided through this very old but well-kept place. It was so colorful with lots of gold and reds and blues. We could not find the children for half an hour. I got a little concerned and prayed that if nothing else they would end up at the van. They were at the gift shop and bought souvenirs. Manfred was amazed at all the wooden ceilings and how good they still looked. There were beautiful chandeliers in almost every room and marble floors hardly worn. Richard took my camera and took a lot of pictures. We were all amazed at the place. We returned to Munich for one more night and headed north. The next day we read in the paper that there was a huge hailstorm in Munich that damaged many cars. I thanked God for our timely departure. Our next stop was to two famous walled cities, Rothenberg and Dinkelsbühl. It rained quite a bit in Rothenberg. We all walked around the cities on the top of the walls. The children were always buying candy since it was different than the usual brands in the United States.

Coburg, Germany, was our destination. One of our challenges while camping in Europe was that we had to buy our food for the day every day. Often, that was not easy. In most of the towns, you had to go to separate stores for every item. Also, we kept forgetting that on Wednesdays and Saturdays all shops close at 2 p.m. On Sundays, only a bakery was open until 10 a.m. We camped in a campground that had a full restaurant, and we ended up with a great German meal— rouladen, dumplings, pomme frites (french fries), and red cabbage. We were really hungry since we had no lunch. We put up two tents in the pouring rain. We ended up staying in the dining room playing cards and board games and having our private church since it was a Sunday. When it was dark, we went into our tents. In the middle of the night Richard called out, "Mom, wake up, we are floating." It had not stopped raining. Packing wet tents in the morning was no fun. We bought some food in town and also huge sheets of plastic to cover the tent.

Doing laundry on this long vacation with all four children was a big challenge. Some of the campgrounds had washing machines. They took forty-five minutes per load to finish. There were no dryers. We laid and hung wash everywhere and put lines between trees. The girls' jeans were the hardest to get dry.

When we did laundry in the town, we also had to buy more money and bought and wrote postcards and mailed them. Then, we drove to the border crossing to East Germany. It took more than three hours standing in line. There were guards all over with big German Shepherd dogs. There were guards also on watchtowers with binoculars. Several times our passports were checked and there were more papers to fill out. The travel agent would not accept our vouchers. We almost turned back. Then, she called the office in Berlin and found out that we had paid and told us how to do it the next time—as if we planned to come back the next year! Michael really had to go to the bathroom, so I told one of the guards. He reluctantly took him there with the dog. Michael was pretty nervous until he got back. They never checked our luggage. Manfred felt pretty nervous driving there. We got safely to our first stop at the town of Eisenach. It was around 4 p.m., and everyone was getting off work. Most people were walking. There were a few small cars and scooters with two cycle engines too. It was raining and gray. We drove up to Wartburg and had a tour of the old castle were Martin Luther had hidden and translated the Latin Bible into German many centuries ago. Our campground was Weissensee, East Germany, which was hard to find. We finally found someone who knew where it was and gave us directions but no indication of distance. After thirty-five miles, we found it. It was eight o'clock by then. We set up our tents and went to the restaurant, and it was closed already. It was a long day! We were all tired; I was about ready to cry. The camp director offered to give us his own soup and bread rolls, but we could not accept because we were way too hungry. We ended up driving to the closest town and had dinner.

It was still raining when we got back to our tents. It was hard to sleep with the wind flapping the plastic cover on the tent so loud. We heard the guard walking around the tents at night. We were up early, packed up, and drove to the town and stopped at the police station to register. We had to give exact travel plans and then ate breakfast in town. It was strange tasting bread and orange juice. We went to get food at the kaufhaus (grocery store) nearby. It was nearly empty.

It was a long rainy drive to Leipzig via the autobahn for two hours. There the campground had A-frame cabins, and they charged seven marks per person. We were relieved— no wet sleeping bags tonight. We ate in a restaurant in the morning and went on to Wittenberg, East Germany. It was a very polluted area from factories. We stopped to get directions to the Schlosskirche (castle church) where Luther's remains are buried and where he hung his ninety-five theses on the front door of the church. The woman who directed us was very excited about us speaking German and coming from America and started to give us directions when a guard with a dog seemed to suddenly come out of nowhere. She stopped smiling and walked off.

After visiting the church, we went back on the autobahn. We stopped at the "Intershop" where tourists can shop with the Deutsch Marks of the West Germans. The kids bought a few candies. Richard was fascinated that East Germans (the local people) could not shop there with their money. We went back to the same camp after seeing the Lutherhaus and other interesting places, and I gave the children a choice for the next day which was that if they were willing to get up real early, we would drive all the way to West Berlin and have breakfast there. The supper at the A-frame campground was not very satisfying. We spent the evening playing *Pinochle* in the cabin. We got to have breakfast by 9 a.m. after crossing the border into Berlin at the famous Checkpoint Charlie.

This trip was quite an education for our children. They are not really spoiled but were not aware of how God had blessed our lives. Even life in Hong Kong was nothing like that. There is a whole new awareness of what life is like when you have no freedom. We drove on from Berlin toward Hamburg camping again, doing lots of laundry, and sleeping in the by-then dry tents. We just hung out and played cards, read, and went for groceries, and got money and stamps to mail postcards.

Finally, we got to Hamburg and spent time with family. The children did a tour of the beautiful Hamburg harbor. Then, came another reason for this extended vacation which was my parents' fiftieth wedding anniversary, July 26, 1984, at a sailing club. My siblings made a wonderful gold covered program with a lot of songs in it. I got to visit with many relatives I had not seen in years. It was a beautiful day with a fantastic view of the harbor. My parents gave us all real gold coins. My siblings have all used them by exchanging them for dollars over the years; I still have mine. Later, there was a big pork roast made all day in the ground at Quickborn. There were lots of relatives enjoying the feast even with the drizzle rain. I played *ping pong* under the awning with my dad. It was an exhausting day; my brain was on overload, so I could not sleep. We had a lazy day the next day by ourselves.

Our next stop was by ferry to Copenhagen, Denmark. It was a challenge to find a place to stay. Usually, we went to the railroad terminal where they help you find housing, but all the places seemed to be occupied in the close-by areas. Finally, we had a nice place farther away in the upstairs of a house of a teacher. There was plenty of room for all of us. I started looking at the books on the shelf and saw that the language was a real mixture of German, English, and Danish. I thought German had long words but in these books a word can almost take a whole line.

We went swimming and wanted to see the famous mermaid "Langeline," but she was not there. One of her arms had been stolen, and it was being repaired. After a few days of sightseeing, we returned to Hamburg. After a few more stops, we arrived in Frankfurt and returned the Volkswagen bus and were more than ready to go home. We took a flight from Frankfurt to Denver. We rested one night and drove home.

When we arrived at home, a huge sign that covered the whole garage greeted us. A big sign of a "Love Is" character that Manfred liked and cut out of the newspapers, welcomed us home.

What a joy to know you are loved by the people we serve and hold dear. I cried and was so happy and tired too. I felt so blessed to have been able to do this vacation with all four children. The girls left the next day to go back to Portland for school.

As I am writing this and look back and see how God has blessed my life, I can't even begin to describe the feeling, like my heart is overflowing. Why is God so good to me? I saw so much sadness and so many hurting people everywhere, and yet, I feel helpless to change and relieve the suffering. At least I can pray for them, and I know God hears all our prayers, and He is in control of this hurting world.

Just a year later Richard graduated from high school, and after working at Camp Perkins as a counselor for the summer, took off for college at Gonzaga University in Washington. Manfred and I took him up there, and as we left him there and drove away, Manfred was crying. He finally understood what I felt like each time I left the girls in Portland.

Reiner and Ursula - 1984
Christina - August 1984 - August 1985

March 17, 1985 – Eighteenth Birthday of Christina

We settled in at home in Pocatello after our wonderful extended trip to Europe and ending with my parents fiftieth wedding anniversary which left us all exhausted and thankful that we had such a joyous but, also, trying time together. Six people who are that close together for almost six weeks can be stressful at times.

I also remember a time in one of the East German campgrounds when Richard and Dori went to take showers but couldn't figure how to turn them on. There were young people from Yugoslavia trying to tell them how to do it, and of course, they couldn't understand a word they were saying. They never got a shower but kept on imitating the way the language sounded to them and had us all in stitches laughing. With the girls away in college and independent already, I was grateful to God how well we all got along. It is one of the things for which I praise God. Family is everything to me. "God, you are so good to us."

Getting home, we quickly got back in our routines, which I appreciated very much. Then, I got this call from my brother Reiner and his wife, Ursula, asking if I would be willing to have Christina, their seventeen-year-old daughter, for a year. I was shocked at first as she was their only child, and they explained that she disliked school and had been getting into trouble.

The German school system has always been hard for many young people. At that time, elementary schools had large classrooms in rows of desks and seating by the alphabet. The A's are in the three front rows. By sixth grade the smarter kids move up to another school that is more advanced with hopes going forward to become university qualified someday. Others go on in Elementary schools 'til eighth grade and graduate. Girls were doomed to become mothers, and boys went on to vocational school. Well, Christina being a Struckmeyer and always at the back of the class, didn't do well and so felt that she was stupid or dumb. She was not, but she is very much a right-brain thinker and a great artist which was hard to show in that climate of education.

Reiner ran a delicatessen and wine store, and Ursula made all the salads and stuff for the store. At the time, they didn't really have the time to deal with her. I told Reiner that I needed to pray about Christina coming to live with us and shared this with Manfred and the boys. I hardly knew Christina, but I knew she was pretty much raised hanging out in front of their store or alone in the apartment over the store. I had real fear because she was six months older than Richard and a beautiful girl, and I also had Michael. What influence would she have on my boys? On the other hand, I also knew she really needed some boundaries, and she was family. Manfred and I prayed about it, and I decided I would share what we would expect of her and that she would have to live by our family rules, and I quoted the rules that were non-negotiable, and they were: she must attend church, go to youth group events, join our prayer time, and do chores by sharing them with the boys. When we called back and told them our expectations, I was thinking they would say that it was too much. I reminded them to be honest and make sure Christina was in full agreement with those expectations as I don't remember if they had asked her about living with me before they called me.

In August of 1984 she arrived. I told her she would have to go to school and took her to register her in the local high school. Since she had English in school, she already knew quite a bit, but speaking it took a little longer. After we communicated quite a bit in German, I said that she must speak in English after the first week. Actually, I was often the one who broke the rule. God had been good to me because Christina, not only a very beautiful girl but also not afraid to try everything, could laugh at her own mistakes. She was very outgoing, so she quickly made friends. She pretty much followed all the rules, but as the year moved on, I was not always aware of everything that was going on. I often prayed that God would please take care of Christina and my boys. It was a big responsibility, but God gave me peace about it. I think girl are harder to raise, and she was not my daughter but my niece whom I love like my own children. All around, it was a beautiful year.

At that time, the church had a youth group in the winter and did a retreat at Camp Perkins. It had no year-round camps like they do now. We used two cabins, numbers five and six. The cabins each had a wood stove, and we heated them with wood that was cut and available in the cabins. We had to hike and ski two miles in with our belongings on a sled. We carried our own food and water. The kids loved it. They played broom hockey on the frozen lake. We did Bible studies, and everyone was helpful, and two nights of this was fun. The day we hiked back out was a blizzard. The Galena Summit was closed. We ended up with one more night at Smiley Creek Inn which they opened up for us. We slept on the floor in our sleeping bags.

The next day, we followed the snow plow out to Challis, Idaho, since Galena was still closed. It was a long stressful drive along the Salmon river 'til we got to highway 93 which was in better shape. We spent a lot of time praying for God's protection. It was a very scary time. Christina had been such a great trooper as was Richard in the boy's cabin.

In March, my brother Reiner and Ursula came to visit for Christina's eighteenth birthday. We had a party at the house and then the youth group had a party at church also. I was relieved to know that we had no real problems and that Reiner and Ursula were so happy to see Christina so loved and accepted by everyone. We still had a few months left 'til she went back ;but overall, it was better than I had feared. I now love her like one of my children. I told her that I'm writing a book of my life, and I wanted to make sure it was okay to use her name in it. She said that year was the best of her life so far. She is married and now lives in Florida. She also has an interesting life now and appreciates how God changed her future after the year with us in Pocatello.

Visits from Friends

In July 1986, my girlfriend Marianne from Germany who I wrote about earlier, came to visit with her son who was sixteen and included his friend. That was a hard week. I had to work my three days during the week, so I could have four days off together. Manfred suggested we go to the World's Fair in Vancouver, Canada. I've never been to one before and looked forward to it. We took the Volkswagen Camper, and Manfred got a bed and breakfast for Marianne and the boys. We slept in the camper there. We all went to the Expo, and I really enjoyed it. But for many things you had to stay in line to get in, which I expected with so many people.

We had allowed for another day at the fair, and Marianne said that the boys and she would just stay at the bed and breakfast. I said to her that you can't do that because people expect you to leave during the day. The owners lived in the house and opened it to renters because of the fair when extra places were needed, so I decided we were driving home the 800 miles, and we did it.

I think Manfred had spoiled them by touring around Yellowstone and the Tetons and the hot springs in the Pocatello area, and she said they decided they were going to cancel their planned trip to San Francisco and stay with us. I don't get angry often, but that was not what I wanted to hear. She was there for two weeks already, and Manfred had his office in our downstairs family room. He had shared with me that she was parading around the house and lying out in the sun with just the pant part of a bathing suit, so he had to work from church where he kept getting interrupted and didn't get much done. Also, when she first came,

I had told her that she could use the car in front of the house—the one that Michael used. He was in Minnesota for a month to visit relatives. I showed them where the stores were and Sizzler where they could eat. I got home and she said to me that Manfred never made us any lunch so wanting to stay with us for me was out of the question. I said, "Your flight from Salt Lake City is in the afternoon. I will take you there tomorrow morning leaving at 8 a.m., so be packed and ready." She thought the world owed her everything because her husband died at a young age with a massive brain bleed. I felt bad for her, but not that bad! It kind of ended our friendship.

That same year, September 21, 1986, through October 2, 1986, we had a much more wonderful vacation in Hawaii for our twenty-fifth wedding anniversary which was in June, but we celebrated it at that time in Maui. The hotel even gave us the honeymoon suite because it was not occupied, and they already received flowers and a big basket of fruit from the members of Grace Church. This was better than our little honeymoon after our wedding in New Jersey. We spoiled ourselves. We swam in the ocean two to three times a day, went into the pool, used the hot tub in our room, ate every meal in the hotel or other restaurants, rented a car to drive around to the other side of the island, and went up to the volcano mountain. I loved to watch the sailboards colorful display as the wind moved them around.

It was a very relaxing and wonderful time with the sensitive, loving man whom God had given to me, because he has made me who I am today.

We have also been on several vacations to Mexico. Our first trip was to Acapulco for five days, and it was an adjustment because I was not very familiar with Mexican food and mostly ate a big breakfast. Manfred loved all the seafood. I was used to Chinese food, and it took me a while to try different dishes. I really don't have many memories of our time there.

The previous year in April 1995, we went to Mazatlan, Mexico, and I have good memories of that visit, partially because on TV, we saw the pictures of the Oklahoma bombing on CNN. It became quite the conversation everywhere. I also really enjoyed walking on that beach and swimming in the ocean. I even enjoyed more of the Mexican food by then. I just could not eat that much cilantro in it; to me it tasted like soap water.

Death of a Relative

Martin, Manfred's brother, who is two years older, and his wife, Barbara, had three children. The oldest was a boy named Andrew who was mentally handicapped. The two younger children were girls. They were in the same age range as our girls, Margarete and Dorothy. They were always our best hosts when returning to Hong Kong after each furlough.

On Easter Sunday in 1989, we got a call from Martin saying that Barbara had died that morning of a massive hemorrhage of the brain. Manfred said right away that he would have to go there. I said that I was going with him, and he was thankful that I made plans to get the time off.

They lived in Palo Alto, California, so we drove there, spending one night in Elko, Nevada, on the way. We were thankful to God to know Barbara was not suffering. We knew she loved the Lord Jesus and were happy to be of support to Martin and the children. Andrew was beside himself. His mom was so good at caring for him. I was also thankful that Margarete was able to come from Seattle, a ten-hour drive. While we were there, we stayed at a Motel Six and other family members were able to come also. The funeral was in the Lutheran church where they were members and attended weekly worship. Barbara was very active and also helped care for a lady who was a quadriplegic in an electric chair. She organized people who would go and help her and bring meals to her. This woman had a handicap van and could drive herself to places, but still needed constant help and had some professional help, as well. She also sang in the choir with Barbara.

I remember feeling so sad after the service because Barbara's name was barely mentioned. This was a very conservative Lutheran church that always feared that if you give someone credit, it would cause pride and "pride comes before a fall." Manfred tried to cheer me up and said that I needed to understand that some pastors fear criticism for not being in God's word. They are stuck. I still felt really sad.

It was really the first time that I was aware that I was never able to be present for my siblings when my father died in 1986 and my mother in 1987. My father died in New Jersey of a massive heart attack while visiting my brother, K-H, and my mother died a year later in Hamburg after suffering from stomach and pancreatic cancer. My youngest brother also died from lung cancer. He was quite the smoker and enjoyed his beer. It made me think how hard it was being so far away from my family. I was happy we could spend some time with Martin and the children before heading home again to Pocatello.

River Float Trips in Idaho

Idaho has such a great variety of places to see and things to do from the high desert, to the mountains, and many lakes and green forests. The Salmon River runs through the middle of the state into the wilderness area. One year, in 1990, for my birthday surprise, Manfred had made a reservation with a professional rafting river company to run the main Salmon River. He knew I loved and had talked about wanting to see the area. He is not crazy about water and so that was such a wonderful gift he gave me. We went in July when the water is not so cold and so fast. It was so much fun. The company had everything supplied, the food, tents, and waterproof bags for our belongings. That way we could just enjoy each day by stopping every day for lunch, camping on beaches in the afternoons, and setting up our tents for the day. In the afternoons, I relaxed by floating on the river in my lifejacket praising God and thanking him for this wonderful creation he made for us to enjoy. On that trip was a group of square dancers from California, and they would dance in the evenings.

I had done the float trip with the youth on the Snake River, which was fun, but a lot of responsibility with children just for two days, but this was a seven-day trip through forests and old homesteads along the way. It also had some hot springs to enjoy in the evenings. There is no access to most of the area by car, but there was one area that had an airport that we floated by. We saw black bears and goats in several areas. Some of the men went fishing along the way, too. One of the rafts had all the food and supplies. I think there were six or seven boats. Bill Bernt (no relation), the owner of the company, caught a seven foot sturgeon, and Manfred took pictures of it before Bill let it go.

Bill and the six-foot Sturgeon 1990

Another time, we floated the middle fork of the Salmon River with a group from our church in Pocatello. This was almost exactly a year later in 1991. It was much more work since the women on the trip had to do all the planning and purchasing, packing and marking everyday meals (three a day), and an afternoon cocktail hour and snacks. Jack and Katie had a float boat, and we got two others from friends. They did the application for a permit, and only fifteen could be in a group. We had to bring our own tents. It was such a fun trip. They also had two inflatable kayaks. The water was much rougher, and everyone had some spills, but no one was hurt. Manfred was really scared through some of the big waterfalls but held on tight, so we got through them. He was holding his breath the whole time. One boat from another group got their raft stuck on a big rock in one of the falls, and we had to help them.

Yet again, not one of them had more than some scrapes and bruises. Before the waterfalls, we had to raft through, we stopped each time and scouted them—like the early explorers had to. This in itself raised the adrenalin in anticipation of having to go through them (portaging was not an option). At night, there was a lot of storytelling and poetry reading, and laughing and singing.

Each vacation was so different, and I am amazed that I was always more than happy to be home again and begin the routine of everyday life. I adjusted well, even with the many changes on our trips. One dream I still have was to be able to float the Colorado River though the Grand Canyon, but it never worked out, and now, I am too old.

Second Trip to Hawaii, China, and Hong Kong – October 1991

Our trip started with the first week spent with our daughter, Margarete, on Maui Island, where she was teaching in the Lutheran School. It was a time to relax and Manfred was reading the book, *Honest to God? Becoming an Authentic Christian,* by Bill Hybels. Manfred shared with me how much he gleaned from that book to share with the congregation when we got back. He was always open to learn, which I thought was great. I walked along beaches, went to "farmers' market" for fresh fruit for breakfast and snacks, and we ate dinners with Margarete.

We flew to Beijing, the capital of China, on a Russian airliner. You could hardly see any lights flying over China. At the airport, we met our group of twelve, all from the United States. We were told not to take pictures of any airports or of military personnel. The group leader had our visas to enter the country. Our hotels were sumptuous with huge lobbies. For the Chinese government, this was important to attract overseas money. Building costs, they said, was one twentieth of what it would cost in the States. In Beijing, we visited the "Forbidden City"— some 2,000 acres of palaces, courtyards, temples, and tombs. There were so many temples, but we were more interested in seeing communities, hospitals, schools, and Tiananmen Square. We saw the square but could not get in to see the Mausoleum of Mao Tse Tung because it was crowded with people standing in lines five deep and a block long.

There were also many school children. I noticed they all looked clean and tidy in their school uniforms. There were usually thirty kids per classroom, and only three or four of them were girls. There were very few cars but thousands of bicycles. The city had a population of eleven million at the time, and there were seven million bicycles. Pedestrians had no right-of-way, so watch out! Then, we walked on the very impressive "China Wall." It was very steep where we were and just packed with people.

We were advised not to drink the water from the faucets. The water bottles in the room refrigerator cost $5 for the small size and up to $25 in the store for larger ones. We were used to that in Hong Kong, but there we boiled all of our drinking water. Our second city was Xian which is more than six hundred miles southwest of Beijing. China is much larger than the United States.

As we were landing there, we noticed how polluted the air was. This area is known for the beginning of the "Silk Route" to the West through the Mongolian desert. We could see many cornstalks on fire because they burn the fields. No wonder the air is so bad because coal is used for everything. We tried to take a walk from one of the hotels, but after less than a block, we turned around because you couldn't breathe. No wonder everyone was wearing masks, because the busses and trucks have no emission controls. Twelve of our fifteen in the tour group had throat problems, including Manfred.

All our meals were always in local restaurants around a fifteen-man round table with a turntable (lazy Susan) for the various dishes. All was ordered by the local guides for the group. Only for breakfast in the hotels, we were on our own and had European-type food.

We ended up writing a lot of postcards in the evenings. You could buy postcards but had to buy a bundle of twenty cards, no single cards. So we wrote a lot. We could not choose specific ones— you get what you get!

In Peking (also named Beijing), we saw Pizza Hut and Kentucky Fried Chicken, which is all new now that China was importing again.

The English version of the *China Daily* talked mostly about some aspect of business, labor, and efficiency in materialism. Their economy was booming in the cities only. Xian is best known for the recently discovered burial ground of some 6,000 life-sized, terra cotta figures of soldiers to "protect" the emperor after he died—an incredible sight.

From Xian, we flew to Shanghai and stayed at a JC Mandarin Hotel. It is China's most Westernized city and Cantonese is spoken here like in Hong Kong. Manfred tried to persuade our Shanghai tour guide to take the group to a *church with no name* because the people there were still fearful of government rules. All the people were from different faiths, and they all had to be in agreement or no deal. Seven were Catholics, one was a Seventh Day Adventist, and a Jewish couple. They were all in agreement since we had all become friends. The church had no denomination—just Christian.

Churches during the Cultural Revolution (1975-1985) had all been desecrated, used by high schools for a while, and then as storage facilities. Pastors had to go work in factories. Now things had changed and the church they took us to had a membership of over 5,000 with services on Sunday mornings, afternoons, and evenings. It had gained 300 members just in that year. Two hundred more were waiting for training in baptism. Manfred asked the pastor a pointed question about the freedom of religion. The pastor said that street preaching, or preaching in public places, or tract distribution, or one-on-one evangelism was not allowed. When friends share with friends, that became the most powerful method of evangelism at that time. After a time, the Hong Kong Oratorio Society was allowed to perform the "Messiah" in Shanghai. The one point the pastor made, at the time, was that the Christians are known to be good citizens.

We also visited some factories, and I got to visit a hospital. That was a sad and shocking experience—so primitive and very dirty. All the work areas were very crowded and close together with poor lighting and no ventilation, and no fans. Every person looked sad; no reaction to our visits and no smiles.

Of course, everywhere we went after each tour, we were taken to the places where they sell their goods. Several couples bought beautiful carpets to be sent to their homes.

Our forth city was Guilin, in the South. This area is famous for its uniquely-shaped mountains. All of them looked like half cucumbers sticking up vertically. Most Chinese paintings are inspired by those mountains. We took a 5-hour boat tour down a river. Our tour guide on the boat was a beautiful girl, and I noticed she was wearing a cross, but she said she was not a Christian. Manfred shared his life as a minister in Hong Kong and shared the gospel with her. She was very fashion conscious and openly shared with the group about wanting to leave China to get into fashion design.

That evening, we saw a half-hour film of how fisherman train cormorants to fish for them. Cormorants are like large ducks but far more aggressive and speedy swimmers. The fishermen tie a collar around their necks and starve them during the day. At night they take about five of them on their 2' by 20' bamboo barges. The birds dive in and swallow the fish, but it can't go down beyond the collar. Then, they jump on the boat and the fishermen grab them by the neck which causes them to spit out the fish into a large basket. The birds can only swallow the small fish—quite an interesting way to go fishing.

The last city in China was Guangzhou, also best-known as Canton. It had become a more bustling city and the many small farms all looked a luscious green. From there, we took the train to Hong Kong. It's just a three-hour trip. On the train, I saw the first use of cell phones which surprised me. At the border of Hong Kong, the police checked under the trains with flashlights to make sure no people were trying to escape into Hong Kong.

Since we had only Chinese meals on the whole trip, most of our group rushed to McDonalds! Manfred and I went to our favorite French restaurant. Then, we stayed with friends who encouraged us to go to each place that we started in the area since Manfred felt he really never said a proper good-bye when he left Hong Kong in 1977. It was a hard decision, and we prayed about it, and Manfred was moved to tears realizing he needed to do this.

Our first visit was with A-Fong. All her children had been successful, and she took us on the new subway to visit some of them. Her husband had died. She was so happy to show us how proud she was of the children's success. Then, we had meals with many Chinese pastors and school principals in various areas. We visited all the places with locals taking us and also went to church in Repulse Bay. There were so many good-byes that it was tiring and wonderful at the same time. One of the joys, even with all the stresses, was that the church kept growing, and more of the schools were also teaching in English. The last night we went to a concert of the Hong Kong Oratorio Society singing Mendelssohn's "Elijah." What a great ending this was for us with all the powerful words in this piece of music.

On October twentieth via United Airlines, we were ready to fly back to Shelton, Washington, to Margarete's home and then drive home to Pocatello. It was a great trip, but I am always thankful to God for the wonderful opportunity to return safely to the comfort of home.

Blessings for Our Children

In 1998, for Richard and Carrie's tenth anniversary, we took them to Cabo San Lucas because that became my favorite place. We had been there a couple of years before. I love the whole atmosphere in that area. Walking through town, and going on a boat with a glass bottom, and seeing the fish swimming by was exciting. They also loved going there and had a great break from children and work. Carrie's mother took charge of their home. Years later in 2002, Harold and Margarete also went there for their tenth anniversary. I had one more trip to "Cabo" with a friend for a "Destination Wedding" of some of my friend's daughters. The date was November, 2013. I was sick with dysentery and fainted during the wedding. There were two doctors at the wedding. They put me on antibiotics, and I got better quickly.

We had booked another trip to Mexico where some of my best friends had a time share. My daughter was almost due to have her first baby. We checked with her after her doctor appointment, and she said go ahead because it may still be two weeks before the baby would be born. This time we went to Manzanillo and stayed high up in a beautiful apartment. We barely got settled, and we got a call that baby Emma was born on February 16, 2002.

We went shopping and did our own cooking. We played card games, but the most fun activity was snorkeling and watching all the colorful fish along a rocky shore. The men went out on the ocean for a fishing tour, but Manfred got seasick and spoiled the fun.

I just love sunshine and water and just can never get enough. I don't lie in the sun on the beach; that is so boring. For reading, it's too bright, and I get distracted anyway by people walking by and the play of children. I love walking along the beach; it is so relaxing. I never tire of it.

Marriage Encounter Work Weekend and Family Reunions

We had many more trips with Marriage Encounter weekends and District Five reunions and National reunions. On one of these weekends in Montana, we decided to check out Fairmont Hot Springs just fourteen miles west of Butte, Montana. We stayed in their hotel for two nights. As I was sitting on the edge of the hot tub, I said to Manfred that this would be a perfect place to have our small family reunions. There are indoor and outdoor pools and a great slide for our grandchildren and our grown children to enjoy. The seed was planted, and the next year we went with the whole family. We stayed in a suite and a couple more rooms. Richard and Carrie had Eli and Isaiah by then, and Margarete and Harold had Sarah and Joshua. Sarah was seven years old and Joshua was eight months old. It was so much fun. We then agreed we would try this every couple of years to meet there. In the future, we rented condominiums as more children came along.

In the year 2000, we had our first big Berndt family reunion in Louisville, Kentucky, which was organized by Manfred's brother, Leander, and his wife, Joyce. We drove there, also stopping in at Concordia University in Mequon, Wisconsin, for Manfred's fiftieth high school reunion. He was the speaker at this event. Now, we were doing the Berndt reunion every five years in 2005, and in Louisville again, and then in 2010, in Estes Park, Colorado, because we needed a larger place for the ever growing family numbers. In 2015, there was one in Colorado again and this time at Winter Park. This time Michael helped me drive our camper there because Manfred had passed away, and Margarete and the children came with us with their pop-up trailer, and we camped along the way in Utah and Wyoming. It was the hardest one for me since Manfred was not there for the first time. This was our last big Berndt reunion because of Covid-19. The reunion in 2020 was canceled. Now, we do Zoom or Google meets every three months. We had several more trips to Germany, especially after we retired in 2000.

RETIREMENT - 2000

Starting to Think About Leaving and Retiring

Already in the 1990s, we started talking about where we might want to retire someday. We checked out several places in Arizona, and even in May it was already too hot for me. We often visited our friends in Scottsdale in February or March and enjoyed that. Perfect weather and sunshine then— but May—no way—but summer, definitely not!

I was very involved and blessed to do the job with Debbie then but was still always aware that Manfred needed to have more support during our last five years working because he still worked so much. I was still involved with caring for people at work and at church.

One of our hardest working members, I'll call him Ron, had contracted kidney cancer. He was a veteran, and his treatments were done in Washington, D.C., for over a year, so it was back and forth from Pocatello to Washington. At the end, they said there was nothing else left to do. He was sent to the Veteran's Nursing Home to die but ended up in our hospital. They flew him from Washington, D.C., and brought him there. I visited him. He looked so thin and weak, and I asked him about what was going on with him.. He shared with me that he was forced to go to the Veteran's Nursing Home to die. He was so sad because he had a young daughter, and she would not be allowed to visit him there. Out of my mouth came the words, "Would you like me to take you to my home since you have to leave here today?" To my surprise, he started to cry and said, yes. I quickly made arrangements for a hospital bed to be brought to my home and called Manfred. He helped move the regular bed out of the guest room, and with the help of others, they set up the hospital bed. He grew to love Ron, but was not aware of how sick he was.

The ambulance brought Ron to our house, and he got there before I even got home. What I had promised was finally hitting home. Manfred, usually a sound sleeper, could not sleep that night. He never really dealt with very sick people except in a hospital setting. I had given Ron

one of those bells that dinged, the kind that they use in the store if no one is at the desk, and he hit it right after I went to sleep, and I had to get up several times that night. His daughter stayed in the other bedroom. In the morning, I told Manfred to make arrangements through the men's church group to stay with Ron during the night, and help me in the mornings to put him in the recliner in the family room for the day. Ron's ex-wife had been very mean to him and had accused him of molesting his daughter years earlier, so he did not trust women. He was on morphine for pain and would not take it from anyone but from me. I finally convinced him it didn't matter who gave it to him because he should not suffer all day. After that, he would take it from whomever visited as long as the person was a man. I kept a visitor's book for the many people who came to visit. It was like a revolving door, and Ron just loved having company. This got a little harder each day, and pretty soon he could not get out of bed anymore. I gave him a sponge bath every evening. During the night, two or three men were around his bed reading to him from scripture and singing hymns to him. Then one morning after I went to work, they called Manfred from his office downstairs saying they thought Ron was dying. He was surrounded by five men holding hands saying the Lord's Prayer together as he died quietly. What a blessing that was for so many people, but especially, to Ron and his daughter. His memorial service was so packed with the many people who loved and prayed for him through this very difficult time.

In 1991, because of government changes, I made some choices that I was not aware of at the time, but I was also was not aware, at the time, of how good they were. Pastors always got a housing allowance since salaries were not great. Well, this changed. If you didn't have a mortgage and your house was paid for, you could no longer claim a housing allowance. We had planned to pay off our mortgage on our house in Pocatello before we retired, so I took out another mortgage and then bought a piece of property in Hailey, Idaho. I loved this area driving through there to go to Camp Perkins in the Sawtooth Mountains of Idaho so often, and thought it might be a good investment.

Manfred didn't think he needed to retire, but realized as the years went by that the church was growing too much for him to handle anymore. He had hired a businessman to take care of running the church affairs, and the school was well taken care of with an excellent principal and staff which was great. But still so much was left to him, not just daily devotions for the staff, but midweek services, two Sunday services, and the leading of the new membership classes were a lot. He was great at finding out the talents of people and had good conflict management ability, but he practically worked eighty hours a week—faithful by serving God and the people. He did daily hospital visits and visited people who could no longer come to church. He created ministry tapes for the elderly and made visits to many homes. He even bought them tape players if they didn't have them. One of our members faithfully ran copies of the sermons he preached. I could tell that everything was getting to be too much. He would wake up at 4 a.m. and often just tossed and turned in bed trying to get back to sleep.

He still thought he wanted to do something else after retiring and contacted the Northwest District of the Lutheran Church in Portland for possible options. Many options came, but each one petered out for lack of funds. In the spring of 2000, it seemed like God was closing all the doors to options Manfred had begun to think about for serving after retiring from his call to Grace in Pocatello.

The big question was "what do we do next to SERVE God?" I was NOT EVEN CLOSE to sitting in a rocking chair on the front porch or in front of a TV. We knew we needed to move away from Pocatello (for reasons of protocol). Manfred had given notice of retirement two years earlier. God was with us. We "saw His hand," as it were, throughout our decisions. Still, the thought of losing all my friends and church family was very painful. God showed (hinted) to us that we should come to Hailey. That was the last place I thought we would go even though we had a nice piece of property there. We had visited Valley of Peace a couple of times, and I wondered why God would want me to worship with just a handful of people. They had a split in the congregation and really needed a pastor at the time, and we prayed about that, and it just seemed like an answer.

We put our house on the market. It sold BEFORE the sign was even up! God's hand and faithfulness were clearly present. Wonderful friends invited us to live with them in Pocatello for the last three months there 'til our house in Hailey was completed. Since I had bought the property already, I thought that maybe this was what God had in mind for us way back when I had decided to buy the property.

A couple of years ago, we had spent some time with friends in Scottsdale, Arizona, and Manfred thought about going there. We visited several cities in our VW camper at the time and had fun visiting friends also. As I wrote previously, that was in April, and when we were in Tucson, it was one hundred degrees. We ended up staying in a hotel because it was way too hot for camping. That for me closed the option of retiring there, and Manfred agreed with me. I thanked God for the clear decision. So, Hailey was the final option.

We came up here where I live now and checked out the area where our lot was, and I fell in love with that part of town. I never realized how beautiful it was when I bought it. It was the end of a street, and there were fields to the southeast and all the way down to the cemetery at that time. Now, there are a lot more buildings to the east, and our road goes all the way through to the high school.

There was only one house for sale in the area at that time, but it only had two small bedrooms. With our large and increasing family of more grandchildren every few years and Manfred needing an office space that would not work. We had an appointment with a realtor, and she listened to our story and needs, and after awhile, she said that since you have that awesome property, she recommended that we build, and in a very short time, it would increase in value.

I thought we would buy a house and sell the property and our house in Pocatello, and we would not have any debt. This really gave me a hard time to process and asked Manfred what he thought about it. He said that whatever I thought was best to do because I knew more about the finances.

Since we spent a couple of nights at Wood River Inn, we went back to our room nervous and excited about our choices and spent a lot of time in prayer for our answer. I felt a heavy responsibility falling on me. Just then we got a phone call from George Brandon, who with his family, had recently moved to Hailey. He said that he was all excited about us coming to Hailey. He said that Valley of Peace church really needed Manfred because there had been a division in the church, and now they were just a handful of people who worship with a pastor coming up from Twin Falls in the afternoons on Sundays. He also helped us find a builder who used to belong to the church, and his wife was very active before the split. His name was Larry Olsen. He used to be a social worker at the high school but changed to go into construction. He had built several houses in the area.

The next day we went with Larry and his wife, Linda, for lunch at Shorty's in Hailey. Since a house plan came with the property when I bought it, he said that he would love to build our house to the plan I had, but I wanted to make just a couple of changes. He recommended Linda Bergerson, an architect who designed the Valley of Peace Church. In just a couple of days, things seemed to be falling in place—all except a way to get a loan for the construction. After a few banks kept wanting to give us only a thirty year loan, not a construction loan, I talked to my friend who always did our taxes every year, and he helped me get a loan for the construction of the house the way I wanted with the U.S. Bank.

I thank God for George's call that really encouraged Manfred and me and also how He kept on putting the right people in my path to help me make these big decisions. I was very scared by what was coming up.

I was still working 'til the end of June, but we wanted to move up to Hailey after Manfred's retirement in October 2000. Sometimes I woke up in the middle of the night having had dreams about myself not living up to my expectations and leading us astray. The thought of being in debt always scared me, and it took a lot of faith for me to trust that I was doing the right thing and that it was God's will. I know that we have to trust God, and I have often done things and made decisions without even asking God's help and feel he has blessed me anyway. This was a whole new experience for me, and it seemed like it was running away with me. Larry had it all under control (the building permits and so much of what needed to be done). After the ground breaking and the digging and pouring cement for the foundation, I was really getting excited about it all falling into place.

After I retired, I spent a lot of time driving back and forth from Pocatello to Hailey to check on the progress of the house construction. I spent time also with Richard, Carrie, and the grandsons, Eli and Isaiah, and encouraging and praising Larry for the great job they were doing. There were lots of trips to Home Depot to try to see various choices of cabinets and flooring. Shopping is not something I enjoy and I become quite impatient. It makes me feel anxious, so a few times I asked Manfred to come with me. Choosing the right refrigerator, dishwasher, and washer and dryer all seems overwhelming to me.

I really was not aware what a big job it was to build a house. Larry Olsen was a big help in giving us some suggestions, and I thanked him for that, but it still fell on me to make the final choices. Dori, my daughter, helped me pick out the carpet and flooring. Thank God for that! The fun was to see it all slowly come together. It was easier for me to take care of very critical patients than what I was now having to do on the house! God had obviously helped me through all this and looking back now, I loved how it all turned out.

At that time Richard, my son, who was teaching in Twin Falls where he and his wife and two small children lived, needed a summer job. Larry hired him, and through his church, they found a place for Richard and his family to live in Ketchum for the summer. Richard biked daily from Ketchum to Hailey and helped with the framing of the house. He assured me that Larry and his nephew from out East were great workers, and that gave me a real feeling of peace. I felt that Jesus was clearly happy with the choices we made. As the building proceeded, I came up from Pocatello every week walking around and trying to figure out where everything was going to be. It was fun, but by the end of summer, it seemed scary to see how many decisions I still had to make before the time when Manfred retired. I feared that the house wouldn't be ready.

Michael, my youngest son, was living with us after he left the U.S. Navy, and I had to tell him that he would have to make plans to move out of our house in Pocatello by May, so that I could get the house ready for sale. We had lived there for twenty-three years, and I had painted inside a few times. We had also built an addition to the kitchen and added a family room out back of the house in 1995, which was awesome with having a growing family and entertaining our many friends. I also painted the outside of the house just a few years before, but the inside all looked like it needed updating and cleaning by that time. I wanted it really to look cared for. God just seemed to take control of our lives. Michael bought a house on the west side up a hill in Pocatello at the end of a road by a canyon. It was perfect for him because he worked 5 p.m. to 3 a.m. or so in Blackfoot, a nearby town, and slept during the day. It was a quiet street.

One weekend in June, I was at Camp Perkins with our group of Stephen Ministry for a retreat. We were putting the house in Pocatello up for sale that weekend. Our realtor Tammie, was a good friend and a member of Grace Church who I felt we could trust to do the best job for us.

While I was at Camp Perkins, Manfred called and said, as I stated before, that she just sold the house before she even put out the sign. I was shocked and said, "Where are we going to live until October?" God took care of that also. Our good friend, Dr. Don Dyer, said to me that he had told Manfred that we were moving in with them until the house was ready. I asked Manfred how Donna, Don's wife, felt about that and had Don discussed it with her. Apparently, it was fine because we moved in with them, and since we had added another wing for classrooms that had just been finished but not yet needed at Grace Lutheran School, we were able to truck all our belongings into one of the empty rooms 'til we were ready to move, and it was just another blessing from our awesome God.

My Retirement

My retirement in June 2000 was announced a few months before it was to happen, but when the date came closer, I was really not ready. I loved my work and all the people I came in contact with. On the actual day they had a big surprise for me. Every one of my coworkers over the twenty-three years at the hospital and all the other departments helped to make it an unforgettable event. They not only wrote notes and letters but had a party in the dining room in the afternoon and served cake and ice cream. The place was packed with so many people that I hardly knew what to say. My closest coworkers also made a beautiful memory quilt that was presented to me in the evening at a dinner party at a Chinese restaurant. I just couldn't believe all the people who were present, including many of my doctor friends. They wrote a poem about me and set it to guitar music and sang it to me.

Several people shared of how I had been an example to them on how to live a life of a true Christian. Manfred was, of course, invited also, and he never realized how much I was loved by so many people. He couldn't stop talking about it when we got home. I was totally blown away and could hardly stop praying and thanking God for the best years of my life with him and all the people I loved and have prayed for, and with, over the years. Not all the people in my life had it easy, and often shared with me and asked my advice so I could bring their concerns to Jesus. I was always surprised by how patiently my children and Manfred would listen as I shared their joys and troubles at the dinner table.

Manfred's Retirement Party

Manfred's retirement party was a huge affair. The church rented the cafeteria at Idaho State University, and it was a catered dinner. I have no memory of how many people attended, but it was several hundred. They had a program, the choir sang, and the school children presented a drama. I know Manfred had always worked hard and really put himself out to bring people to Christ. He did not stress membership, but because of the way he treated people, many attended his "Basic Bible Truth Class" and became members. The church grew by leaps and bounds over the years, and he never dwelled on that. He was a very humble servant of Jesus Christ and he gave God and all the leaders the credit for its success. I know that I often took it for granted all the time because God had called him and placed him where he was needed. At the big party, many people shared their testimony in becoming worshippers because of his persistence in following up on people who visited.

Just one example is our dear friends, Jim and Sue. They had just come to Pocatello from Kansas. They came to church to visit, stating that they were "church shopping." They were just recently married after she attended the Kansas State University, and she had gotten a job as a professor at Idaho State University. He had a degree in landscape architecture. Jim shared that because Manfred visited them the afternoon after they came to church, and they were so impressed with him, they never went to another church!

I was in tears for most of the testimonies because I realized God was so much greater than I thought He was. It was like I was hit over the head by all those reports of how Manfred had touched people and the results. Lots of people thanked me for allowing him to work so many hours and never complain. It is really all the Marriage Encounter weekends that kept us together and on track to keep on serving.

As I think about all the great events in our lives, I can hardly believe it that God gave us so many blessings. Clearly life is not all roses, but recalling the blessings from God is more fun than recalling some of our own struggles in our years together.

Retirement in Our New Home

After Manfred's retirement, we finally moved into the house in Hailey on October 21, 2000. We only had water in the master bathroom and the toilets. It was hunting time, and the plumber was not available 'til the next week. We made it work. Many people from Valley of Peace church helped us move in quickly. We had amazing helpers from Grace Church in Pocatello to put all our belongings in two moving trucks, and they also drove them up here for us. There were many special prayers and tears as they left taking the trucks back. There were not only their tears, but mine as I cried knowing I had to make all new friends, which is also scary, but really wasn't that hard in the end because of the church members. I've been so blessed all my life with just the right people to guide, help, and support me. I trusted God that He would keep me in His loving arms in this new chapter in my life.

Valley of Peace (Past and Present)

After getting settled into our new home in Hailey, Idaho, it was time for me to decide what I wanted or needed to do with my time now that I wasn't working outside our home. I really wanted to get to know the area we now called home and also to find some friends. It didn't take me long to get to know some of the few, faithful members of the church. They helped me find out about medical care and dental care. I started getting the weekly paper, and we got a post office box because where we lived in 2000 was a pretty new area, and the post office did not deliver there.

More importantly, Manfred visited several people and soon started a new member class Amazingly, we had quite a few attending the group which Manfred called a "Basic Bible Truth Class." It was about helping people to know what a church is about, not so much as members, as getting to know God and His great love for all people. That gave me opportunities to also invite people to my home for dinner to get to know them better. Also, I saw the need to help clean the church weekly and invite someone to help me when possible.

One wonderful person was Lotte, and she loved to hike and knew all the places for the best hikes. We started hiking at least once a week together. Sometimes her husband and Manfred joined us for longer hikes in the Redfish Lake area or even Stanley. I just love it when I come to a meadow, and it is full of colorful flowers. It just filled my heart up with joy to overflowing. One day we were hiking to Prairie Lake and came to such a colorful meadow and Lotte said, "God was here before us." That was so true, and it is so good to think how beautiful God's creation is and how He wants us to enjoy it.

Many of the more local hikes around here I could also do by myself, and for me, it is a feeling of peace knowing God is by my side. One of the closest places to walk is right by my house in Quigley Canyon, and I now walk it most weekdays with Dori's dogs, Bella and Sylvia. It is a wonderful time with God and even some of the other people walking with their dogs.

I also started going to the Bellevue Elementary School to help first graders with reading, and that was fulfilling and good to get some time with the children.

Another person who impressed me right away as a very devoted person who worked for the good of the church was Stacy. She wanted the church to grow by helping with activities that included people, especially children in the community. I soon learned about making gingerbread houses. That was something the church had started some years ago. I saw how she organized it—very impressive.

People baked the shapes from a pattern she gave us at home. Then, she set a date on an evening for us to put the houses together. We made the icing using a mix and a blender and then using the icing to put the house together by putting completed houses on boards she had already ordered. She put an ad in the paper to invite children from the community on Sunday afternoon to decorate the house with candy. We had to make icing for this and ruined several hand and blended mixtures in the process. When I first came to America and worked at the bakery in Staten Island, I know that our icing came ready in big buckets, so I recommended that we should look into that. It sure made it so much more fun doing this activity in future years.

Many families came with their children. I was amazed and saw what an impact this activity had. Manfred walked around to take pictures, which he always did anyway, but he had a devotional time in the church for all who came, as we set up all the houses on folding tables. Also, at an area festival, we had a burrito booth, and we helped with that, which was something I had never done. (*(f) see add. info.)*

2000-2006

I can't believe how much I've already written about my life and all the wonderful people God has put in my life---always at the right time when I needed them. Looking back has really helped me to see God so much more clearly, and how much He loved me, still loves me, and cares for me. Just serving at Valley of Peace part-time was keeping Manfred and I very busy starting with gingerbread house events, two garage sales at church, and a house blessing of our home. Making refreshments for that event involved both Carrie, my daughter-in-law, and Dori who came to help. We had about thirty people celebrate with us, including Larry who built the house and his wife, Linda.

Often we invited visitors to our home on Sundays after church services to have lunch. I started to clean the church every week for a few years, and Manfred cleaned the windows. Before, as I already mentioned, there was a church retreat at Camp Perkins, which was a great experience to also get to know people better.

Manfred still attended the monthly meetings of all our Lutheran churches and pastors in the Magic Valley area every second Tuesday of the month and was on the lay leader ministry committee in Portland to help train more lay pastors for churches who are small and can't afford a full-time pastor. There was a shortage of pastors. The lay pastors are trained and then supervised by the committee or a pastor in the area. So, he often flew to Portland.

In November of 2002, we bought a Roadtrek 1900 and started camping in the valley and the Sawtooth Mountains, often from Sunday afternoons to Wednesday. It was a great time to really appreciate the beautiful area where God allows us to live. It really made our summers a blessing. We always took our bikes. We also had some visits from friends and, of course, frequently our children and grandchildren. What a wonderful way to spend time in our "retirement!"

Hiking became a big part of my life. Manfred spent a lot of time preparing sermons and writing notes to people and visiting. So I hiked with friends but mostly with Lotte, my dear friend from Switzerland. We seemed to have a lot in common. In winter, instead of hiking, it became skiing which was great exercise and fun.

Also, we had a women's Bible study one morning a week, and when it was at my house, I combined it with tying the quilts. I sent many quilts to Lutheran World Federation that would go to the mission fields, but I also brought several to the Boise Rescue Mission on my way to go to Shelton.

I attended the Grace Lutheran Church women's retreat every September at Camp Perkins, which helped me to spend time with friends from the past but also see new members from Grace. I loved that time, and it refilled my "love tank" so much. The weekends seemed to end too fast. We still also had "almost monthly" Lutheran Marriage Encounter weekends to attend.

Twice, we flew to Alaska for a weekend. We stayed at a beautiful hotel, and I was blessed to look out of our window, and Mount McKinley was so clear it seemed it was right near me. They said some people had been there and never got to see it because it's usually in clouds. So, I know we were blessed.

Many weekends were in Idaho, but we also went to Seattle, Philadelphia, Florida, Denver, and Phoenix. Of course, I already mentioned about the convention in Finland which we lengthened with our Germany visit with family events.

The years seemed to pass quickly with Dori and Eric getting married and giving us two beautiful granddaughters. Margarete and Harold added two more boys to their family and now have four children. Richard and Carrie moved to Twin Falls and added four more grandchildren. So, I ended up with ten grandchildren (four girls and six boys). There were lots of busy visits for holidays and in the summer. Most of the children attended Camp Perkins' summer retreats and spent time with us before camp and after.

With all our joys and business, there were also a few sad events. One of our friends got killed in an airplane crash in their own private plane. It took quite a few years for this couple, after attending a Lutheran Marriage Encounter weekend, to become members of the church. Manfred had spent quite a lot of time with them, and they attended his "Basic Bible Truth Class," but always still had questions. This accident happened just shortly after we retired. He was a doctor and often approached me in the hospital cafeteria while I ate lunch and wanted to talk. We grew close to this family. He, his wife, and their son were killed. They left two college-age daughters behind. Manfred did their funeral service in Pocatello. It was so hard on the girls.

Then, every summer we had our Lake Powell trip on the houseboat which we both looked forward to. There were spring visits to Scottsdale with some friends from the houseboat. I still participated in those events even after Manfred died.

Another sad time was when Carrie's parents were killed in a car accident. What a sad time for the whole family and for Richard also. They had just moved to Twin Falls, Idaho, a short time before and enjoyed Eli, their grandson, so much. They were such a wonderful couple who served God all their lives and also left their footprints at Camp Perkins where they spent their summers. She, the artist, painted rocks and signs there. What a sad loss it was. Sometimes I just wonder why God takes these wonderful people away and when it seems to me before their time. I have to remind myself that we do not need to know the answer. He is in control of our lives. "Trust and obey, there is no other way." That song comes to mind, but it is not always easy to do.

Then, in 2001, as I mentioned earlier, we had our first small Berndt family reunion at Fairmont Hot Springs, Montana, in the Montana mountains---which incidentally, we had more Frequently throughout the next years. Those are memorable times for all the children and grandchildren, and there was so much fun playing outdoor games, sharing meals together, and really getting to know each other better. Manfred always did the Sunday service by a lake.

Whenever we went back to Pocatello, we would stop in Carey, Idaho, on the way to give holy Communion to a housebound, widow lady, Edith, who was an active member of Valley of Peace around the time the church was being built.

I also continued with LWML for just a couple of years, but we don't have any active group here; nevertheless, I still fill my mite box and have taken it to Shelton for the group at Margarete's church.

One of Manfred's younger brothers, Ted and his wife, Nancy, invited us to attend their daughter's wedding in Grey Eagle by Lake Tahoe in Nevada. It was a beautiful event and always fun to renew relationships. Then, Paige was born, also Matthew, and our last grandchild, Luke, in those years. We were blessed with ten grandchildren.

In 2004, while Margarete and Harold celebrated their tenth wedding anniversary in Cabo San Lucas in Mexico, we were caring for their children. Margarete and Harold had some rental homes that Harold was remodeling. Manfred was helping when we came. On one of our visits when Margarete was in Seaside, Oregon, Manfred was helping Harold in a remodel, and Harold fell and broke his leg. Manfred panicked and called me. I told him to call 911, explaining that I couldn't help a big man if his leg was really broken, and it was. This was not a simple break of the tibia, and he ended up with surgery and a long recovery. Sometime later he ended up in the hospital again with an embolism to the lungs. God was with him because one of the children he took care of while Margarete was working called 911. Margarete called me at that time and I quickly left Hailey and drove the 726 miles to their house arriving at 1 a.m. in the morning. God was with me during that time. I do not enjoy driving in the dark and prayed the whole way.

We also went to Port Charlotte, Florida, for my brother Karl-Heinz's seventieth birthday celebration where many of my siblings from Germany came. Some of his children and Christina were also there. It is always a joy to be with family to get to share in their lives and They in our lives and dreams. ((g)see add. info.)

Another big Berndt reunion, in 2005, was when we attended and drove our camper there. We stopped in Wisconsin for Manfred's fiftieth graduation reunion, which I already mentioned.

For Manfred, these years were still very busy, until his second retirement, but they were also very fulfilling years. In the Bible, in Ecclesiastes, Chapter 3, there is a section that says that there is a time for everything, a season for every activity under heaven, and it was clear to me that it was time for Manfred to retire completely. We shared about this often. We were ready.

One other wonderful memory is that one year Ted and Nancy joined us on a winter outing to Yellowstone Park. We had a hotel in West Yellowstone and then an event to "Old Faithful" area in a snowcat. That was something new for all of us and so awesome. The area looks different in the winter. We skied cross country to a waterfall. We saw so much wild-life. There were huge elks with big racks, foxes, and one bear who had not yet taken his winter nap. It was great to spend a couple of days there and get to know Ted and Nancy better. Life is often so busy that we don't allow ourselves to really get to know our relatives and also friends. It surely was a very memorable trip.

Meetings at Valley of Peace Church in Hailey, Idaho

A couple came into the church. I did not know them, so I introduced myself. I asked them what brought them to Hailey and the church. They were visiting a daughter and family living just up the street from there. They came from Oregon. They were Lutherans and both were from Lutheran families. As others came into church, I introduced them and left their side to prepare for communion.

After church, as I was cleaning up from communion, this gentleman came in and started sharing with me that his daughter was brought up in the church, too. She was married once and put effort in it for three years to make it work but finally got a divorce. Now she is living with a really nice man but there was no mention of marriage after a few years living together. He said that he had a problem with accepting that.

After a while I just said to him, "All you need to do is love your daughter and let God be the judge."

He just looked at me, and I could see the wheels turning in his mind.

He said, "No one has ever said that to me."

He just hung around after that. His wife was talking to someone else in the narthex.

Finally I said, "I need to get going."

He said that weather permitting they might still be there next Sunday. Clearly, he hoped to talk to me again.

One of My Favorite Vacations after Retirement

One of my favorite vacations ever was our river trip down the Danube River. After visiting family, we flew to Munich on October 5, 2002, and stayed in a nice hotel for three days wanting to experience a real Oktoberfest, only to find out we missed it. That was the last day of all the festivities, and they were starting to take down all the tents. So, we relaxed and did a lot of hiking before a bus took us to where the river trip started. It was called "Blue Danube Waltz." Our ship was called the *River Aria*. All the ships had names that were musical themes.

Our cabin had one round window below the water line. We made many stops in cities along the way. It was a beautiful peaceful fall season with all the colorful glory God created for us all to enjoy. We started in Regensburg, Germany, for two days and ended the trip in Budapest and stayed there for two days in a hotel—all part of the tour. When we stopped in cities, we always went along on the guided tours. We went to an organ concert in Passau. Then, we stopped in Melk, and Dürnstein and Vienna, Austria. In Vienna, they took us to a local restaurant and later to a musical performance. Then we went on to Bratislava, Slovakia, and then on to Kalocsa, Hungary, where we went to a traditional horse show with colorful decorated horses and riders. In the evening was another organ concert. The last stop was Budapest where we disembarked and stayed in the hotel mentioned earlier. It was on a pedestrian-only street and very noisy with singing and partying 'til late in the night. It sounded like everyone was happy. We had a couple more tours of some traditional villages, and on our own, we toured the castles. The city is divided by the river on one side and named Buda and the other side is named Pest. For me, the best part of the whole trip was the wonderful service. The dining room had tables for six people. Since most of the travelers were in pairs, with friends who were in pairs, at each meal we tried to sit at tables with couples we had not met before. It was wonderful getting to know so many people on a fourteen-day trip. I was also fascinated going through all the locks, which were mostly during the night, where we watched the boat go down and then back up. The food and wine, which was included in the evening meals, was good. I just loved the whole trip so much and even now recalling our time together on that tour makes me happy---but also a bit sad.

What a way to start our retirement! On that trip we had so many people we could share our love for God, and the joy Manfred and I had to touch so many people who seemed lost in their lives and seemed to be running away from family and responsibilities.

The Buhler Family and My Roadtrek Camper

For many people, moving to a new place is always scary and stressful. You leave your friends and familiar surroundings behind. You hope you can find new friends, a new dentist, a new doctor, and stores you are not used to, and it can cause anxiety. Belonging is part of what we all need and desire. The blessing for me was that most of my friends were only two-and-a-half hours drive or 156 miles away. Also, the church helped me to feel at home quickly.

One of my new friends was a walker and a hiker. She and her awesome husband were more serious about getting out into nature. They also went backpacking in the mountain north of Hailey. We became good friends, and she acquainted me with all the hikes in the area. It was always a great time to get to know each other better, and I could share my love for God with her. I always looked forward to our time together. Some days when her husband was not working, we hiked together to different mountain lakes in the area north of here. Manfred would join us on those hikes. It was fun to get to know the area with friends.

After two years here in Hailey, we bought a camper, a Roadtrek 1900. It was so much better than the Volkswagen camper we owned years ago in Pocatello. It was a little larger and had a bathroom which was important to me. We often left Sunday afternoons when the tourists left and camped for three or four nights. It was so comfortable with a big bed and all the conveniences it gave us. We mostly camped by the river so Manfred could go fishing, which he enjoyed. We had a bike rack on the back and took long bike rides as well as hikes.

When we built the house, I already had the dream of that kind of motor home, so we built a higher garage and garage door. So after eighteen years, it still looked like new when I finally sold it. Because of COVID, I did not use it for two years, and my children did not like me camping alone anymore. I still miss it, but am happy it went to a lady who will enjoy it because she was retiring that spring from her job at the school.

We sometimes went to Stanley Lake to camp, and since my dear friend moved there and built a beautiful log house after he retired, we hiked to many lakes in that area. When we first came to Hailey, he was the chairman of the little church where Manfred was the pastor part-time, after retiring from Grace in Pocatello. Now, they are still my friends but now mostly on the phone because there was no more cross country skiing and hiking at that time---because of the pandemic. Thank God for times past and cheap telephones.

A Visit from My Great Nephew from Germany

Whenever I've been in Germany visiting the family, we always had a big get-together at a restaurant with a huge dinner. Many of the extended family I barely knew, but it was fun to visit with them and share with them how blessed I am. Even without Manfred, I was blessed to have family close by me. This visit was in March and April of 2011, which would have been my parents one hundredth birthdays because they were both born in March in the same year. My father was eight days younger than my mother. He would say, "Mein altes weib" (my old wife). The family always finds a lot of excuses to have another party, and this one was special because I was coming. One of my sister Hella's grandsons asked if he could come visit me sometime. I, of course, said that he was welcome to come anytime. Hella is the one in the family who always starts planning these get-togethers. I usually stayed with her when I visited.

So in June 2012, Sebastian Ritt came to visit me—a wonderful young man. He wanted to see more of the northwest part of our country. As an exchange student, he spent some time in California, if I remember correctly. Anyway, I let him use my Roadtrek camper and everyone said that I was crazy to let him take it. He was too young to rent a car. I showed him everything he needed to know about the "truck" and told him just one thing—whatever you do, don't hit any people. If you have an accident like a bump on the truck, it's no big deal.

He put four thousand miles on the camper with no problems. He camped mostly by Manfred's relatives on the way to Reno, Nevada; Palo Alto, California; and Portland, Oregon. Then when I went to Margarete's in Shelton Washington, I met him there. I told him to get an oil change for the camper at Walmart and then after visiting a few days there, he continued up to Vancouver, Canada, and I came back to Hailey.

At the end of his trip, continuing from Vancouver, Canada, he went through to Banff, Jasper, Edmonton, and then down to Bozeman, Montana, in the US, then Yellowstone, the Tetons, and back home. It was quite an adventure.

May 2017
Addition of Another Dog to Walk

That year Dori and Eric also got a second dog, a labradoodle. It is gray-black (sort of silver color) and so cute. They named her Sylvia, and now I had two dogs to walk. Thankfully, Bella trained her, and even today, she is so much fun.

The Birches – Then and Now

Some of the couples we presented Lutheran Marriage Encounter with over many years have become our very best friends and are still mine now. Fred and Gale Birch always invited us to spend a week on the houseboat with them. Many time we could not because of other plans or travels. It's like a timeshare, and they assigned weekends because there are six owners. One year we finally got to go, and it was so wonderful that it became an annual event almost every year. For me, one of the favorite things was that we usually knew most of the people they invited. There was a lot of family, so I got to know their children really well within the week or ten days we spent in close company. Also, I only needed to bring food for one whole day which was breakfast, lunch, cocktail hour, and dinner. One day you were the slave. The rest of the time you enjoyed other people's cooking.

Each day or two, you stopped at different beaches after travelling up river on Lake Powell. Manfred enjoyed the fishing, and I loved the swimming. In the early mornings the lake was like glass, and I would dive off the back deck and swim until the sun came up and then head back to the boat which was the best time of the day for me. Manfred did morning devotions every day when we all were done with breakfast.

As the years went by, the grandchildren started to come along, and I helped with caring for them. It always felt we were just one big family together. We had wonderful memories over the many years we spent. As we retired, we usually went in late August and September, and there were usually four couples. Manfred and I usually had the most private room which gave us some time alone also. But after Manfred died, I got to share that space or sleep in the living room which was fine with me. This was one of my favorite things every year, and the close relationship with this family is one of the most precious things in my life.

This is one of the many blessings of Marriage Encounter. There are couples I meet at times when shopping down here in Twin Falls, Idaho, (about sixty miles from Hailey) who recognize me and share how we saved their marriage and how they are active in their churches.

God really blessed us by allowing us to share God's love through this miracle of LME (Lutheran Marriage Encounter) that really changed our lives and our marriage way back in 1977. We were so busy that each of us went our own way. Yes, we were each serving the Lord, but we were like two ships going in opposite directions. It helped us so much also in our relationship with our children.

After both of our retirements, I visited them in Scottsdale twice a year for many years. Finally in May 2017, the Birches came to visit me. We attended some of the symphony concerts in Sun Valley together. It is just so enjoyable to host people you love.

So the years just flew by with visits from Sebastian again for snow-boarding in winters and my niece, Jutta, in September of 2019, for three weeks visiting the Tetons, Yellowstone, and staying at a friend's beautiful "cabin" in Swan Valley at night. It was fun sightseeing and hiking with her, and we took a river rafting trip together. That was a blast. Of course, we did some sightseeing in this beautiful area as well. Cooking together was an extra bonus.

A Visit from My Niece and Her Daughter - 2019

My niece, Claudia, from Germany, and her daughter, Luna, came to visit me over the Christmas holidays for just over a week. That was great because she and Emma and Paige really had fun together, and she got to see more of my family since we congregate here for the holidays. They went to Christmas Eve services with us and enjoyed it. At the beginning, Luna seemed very shy, but it didn't last long before she had more confidence speaking English.

ABOUT MY CHILDREN

Weddings

I am very proud of all our children, and we were able to attend all their graduations, weddings, and special events. I have hardly mentioned them at all. Dorothy was the first one to get married, as I already mentioned earlier. She had a big wedding in the old church downtown. Manfred did the ceremony. My parents came for that wedding and my dad walked her down the aisle. He wrote her a long letter saying that she needed to start having children right away, which Dorothy did not really understand at the time. To him, it was so important that the Caucasian race grow fast. In his heart, he was still thinking that Hitler's idea of sterilizing all black people in Africa and the world was the right thing to do because Caucasians are the only smart people according to his belief of white supremacy. It was a good thing they never had children because she knew she married the wrong man right from the beginning and endured it for five years because she feared what our reaction would be about divorce, especially her dad because he married them.

Richard and Carrie's was the first wedding performed in the new church, Grace Lutheran Church in Pocatello. They were still quite young too, but it just seemed like they belonged together from the start. Both came from great Lutheran church backgrounds, and it was a big wedding too. We all worked together on it since her parents were church workers and the funds were limited. It was a beautiful wedding. Manfred married them, and Carrie's parents and brothers and sisters were all present. The reception was right at the school gym by the church. The church was packed with people. There was a lot of work that went into this event, and I could not imagine what it would have been like if we didn't have so many friends and family to help. It was a New Year's Eve wedding, and we had a lot of snow and cold weather.

The next big wedding was Margarete's and Harold's in Olympia, Washington, on April 23, 1994. The tulips were in bloom everywhere, and we had beautiful, sunny weather. Since Margarete was teaching in Lacey at the time, her children from school sang at the wedding. Many visitors came from the extended Berndt family too. The reception with a catered dinner was in a different place, but we all decorated the hall the day before the wedding. Harold had bought a house in Shelton, Washington, earlier. Margarete lived in a condo she bought a couple of years before in Lacey, Washington.

Then in February 2001, Dori and Eric got married in Twin Falls in a small wedding chapel this time. They had a nice reception in a hotel. By then, Margarete had two children, and I remember how cute they were when they danced at the reception. After meeting Eric at our home in Pocatello, she then moved back into Idaho from California. She loved her life in California, but she got homesick for her family. Her relationship with Eric, who she met earlier at our home, became more serious, and I was happy that she was ready for this exciting event of the wedding.

Margarete, Dorothy (Dori), and Richard (Chard)

It just occurred to me that my daughter Margarete is just like me. She knows what she wants and goes after it. During her life she had special friends, did her own travels, and enjoyed life one day at a time. She became a teacher and taught school in Hope Lutheran School in west Seattle, on Maui Island in Hawaii, and then in Lacy, Washington. She met Harold, and they moved to Shelton, Washington, where she had four children and built onto a small house. They still live there, serving God by running a preschool at Mt. Olive Lutheran Church and School. She is a wonderful mother and sings in a church band and plays the guitar. She loves family activities and is always coming home for special events and, especially, to our small Berndt family reunions, as well at the big Berndt reunions.

Dorothy (now Dori) is another story. I often think that God gave her to me to keep me humble. She is the one who tested all the rules, and she was in my prayers for the teenage years. She went to Concordia, Portland, for one year, but she didn't really know what she wanted to do. She had spent a year at home and went back to college again. She didn't really want to be a teacher because Margarete was, but in the end, she did become a teacher after realizing that while working as a helper in a private preschool in Portland, she did most of the work, and the teacher got the pay. She ended up finishing her teaching degree at Concordia University in Portland. Then, she moved to Los Angeles and started teaching there. She had divorced her husband after a few years and started a new chapter in her life. She also went back to school at UCLA in California to get her masters and continued for a lot more education.

Richard, my other son, also graduated at seventeen from high school and worked summers at Camp Perkins. He never had a job while in school because all his energy went into running both track and cross country. He also played soccer for a while and basketball, but they interfered with his first love—running. While in school in Pocatello, he had mononucleosis, and while he was home, he taught himself to play guitar which helped while working in the summer. Their cross country running team won the state meet one year and had set a new record, which after ten years, was still there.

All of our children were active in church and youth groups. One of the most important things was our dinner at nights together for most of their childhood. What I loved about Richard was that he almost always stayed at our house, and all his friends came to us. I never worried about him or his faith which he shared freely. Even when he went to college in Gonzaga in Spokane, Washington, I almost always got lengthy, weekly letters from him. After two years, he transferred to Boulder, Colorado, to continue his education in engineering. He worked at a Perkins restaurant as a cook to earn an income. He also met the love of his life the next year, while working at Camp Perkins in Idaho for the summers. *((h) see add. info.)*

Michael - My Adopted Son

I have been so blessed and also learned so much by having Michael in our family. He seemed to be a very happy child and I can see that in our many pictures we have of him. We raised him the same way we raised our other three children.

As he grew up and was ready for school, I became more aware of the fact that something was different. Since our trip from San Francisco to Seoul, Korea, on one of our furloughs from Hong Kong, I noticed he slept the whole time. I noticed that even now as an adult, he still likes to sleep during the day.

In the Beacon Hill School when we still lived in Hong Kong and where the girls also went to school, I think it was the only school where he truly loved his first grade teacher because she seemed to understand him much better than I did. I remember the time after morning recess, she handed him a book and told him to go to the reading corner and let him sleep for twenty minutes. She said that he would participate in learning better. I remember the girls making fun of him because if we were going anywhere in the car, he would be in the back sleeping. We had one curving, winding street to go up to get to our home, and the kids all said to me that he falls asleep on the wiggly street. That made everyone laugh, but it was true.

When we went to church in Repulse Bay on Hong Kong Island, it was always a long drive around the mountain and onto the ferry to get back home. Many times after leaving church, I often jokingly asked, "Where is Michael?" He usually popped up his head. Well, this one time it didn't happen— no Michael popped up. We had to drive back to church, and there he was with a bunch of teenagers smiling. He never realized we had left.

In Pocatello, he went to school at Grace Lutheran School and started second grade, and he seemed to do all right. By third grade he was not keeping up, and the teacher never said anything to us until the end of the year. From then on he struggled, and it made me realize how important third grade really was. He made it through school and graduated but never really loved it.

He is very bright and tried one year at Idaho State University, but he felt they tried to teach stuff he didn't need and didn't like. He quit and worked in two places instead. He liked Chinese food. because even in Hong Kong, he often preferred eating with our amah, A- Fong. He even helped the Chinese restaurant with advertising. I prayed about what his future would hold and finally told him that we love him but that he needed to grow up and have a plan of sorts because by his twenty-first birthday. He needed to be out of the house. In 1999, and just in time, I saw a note on the kitchen counter, and it said that he was in Salt Lake City entering the U.S. Navy for submarine training. Even though Michael had trouble reading when young, he was an avid reader of science fiction books, and that was what he was able to enjoy while in the Navy. It seemed like an answer to prayer that he found an avenue that fit his personality. Thank you, Jesus, was all I could think of.

Michael's basic training was in Great Lakes, Illinois, north of Chicago. We were so happy to know God was with him and helped him to do so well. Since Manfred's oldest brother lived in River Forest, Illinois, we decided we could go to the graduation since we had a place to stay in the area. Hans and Erma welcomed us and went with us up to the graduation. Hans is Manfred's oldest brother and ten years older. He taught Spanish at Concordia University.

While driving there, I prayed that Michael really had found what he loved and to be able to use his gifts. Sitting on the bleachers and seeing all the young men in full uniform was beautiful. It looked like a white wave coming in and lining up. I had no idea there would be so many young men at that place. I had no idea which one of those handsome people was Michael. All had the same haircuts it seemed, and it also seemed they were all six feet tall. I was so thankful and overwhelmed by the whole function that I had goose bumps the whole time and looked forward to actually seeing Michael and understanding how this affected him. I prayed that this was what God had guided him to do. I could not imagine me in a confined space like a submarine but could see how that might fit his personality.

In Groton, Connecticut, they received the technical training. They went to many ports, but most of the time, they just floated in the ocean. I asked him how he spent his time there. He said it was all divided into three eight-hour shifts. He was on duty for eight hours and was on assignment to communications where he was mostly on his own. He learned how to fix all the equipment, and how it all works, and fixing what was not functioning correctly. This was right up his alley, and he loved it. Praise God! Everything was a secret. If someone asked what were the plans for getting into a port, he was the right person to be able to keep secrets with a smile. I wanted to hear what he did the other sixteen hours. There was some technical training, exercises, meals, and then sleep for eight hours. There was no bedrooms. There was just a place that was empty to crawl into to sleep. I think they must have had personal lockers.

He spent five years in the submarine and visited various places like San Diego, California; the Great Lakes in Illinois; Norfolk, West Virginia, and even rode through to the Panama Canal and had a barbecue on the top of the submarine. In all the years he was gone, I received only one letter, and I still have it. While he was in San Diego, he sometimes visited Dori who was living and teaching in Los Angeles. One time a big earthquake hit the area in 1994 or 1995, and they woke up. Dori called me very early in the morning to say that she was so scared and standing in the doorway. She said that Michael was holding the television so it wouldn't fall. In that scary moment, I was praying for them when our electricity went out, too. It was a very scary time for them, and Michael couldn't get back to his base for a bit.

Michael left the Navy in 1996 and came back to Pocatello. He got a good job that fit him perfectly in a potato factory in Blackfoot, Idaho, on a late shift as an office manager. He loved the hours and dealt with the many drivers who came to truck the produce all over the country, and all the day people appreciated his efficiency, positive outlook, and smiles.

In 2011, they had a big fortieth birthday party for him with our help. It was so much fun. Sadly in 2013, the company in which Michael worked, "Nonpareil," sold the business and let Most of their workers go and brought in their own people. That was very hard on Michael. He enjoyed the people he was working with, and those were the best hours of the day for him since he has always been "a night owl."

A Miracle Happened

Michael had a job that was perfect for him for all those years after he left the Navy. Then, as I said before, the company he worked with was sold. He lost his job and had no luck getting another job for several years and finally lost his house. Of course, Michael really never shared his predicament with me when he came up and visited for all the holidays. Then one year he did not come up for Easter, stating later that he was in Salt Lake City to get his commercial driver's license (CDL) and was going to drive trucks. After not answering any emails or phone calls from me, I really started to be concerned. I had been praying for him to get a job all along but felt something was not right. His friends also let me know that they hadn't heard from him; then, I really started to pray. I was in Pocatello and called him, and that was when he said he was in Salt Lake City. Grace Lutheran School had a fundraiser the first weekend in December that year, so I was in Pocatello staying with Jim and Judy. Dori was in Pocatello where Paige had a volleyball competition and couldn't find him, so I went to his house. There was no answer to my knock. I walked around the house and everything was locked. Peeking around the back, I noticed his plant in the window looked healthy. I tried the garage entrance number, but it did not work. The front screen door was locked, so I finally left.

That same week, we started having Wednesday evening Advent services, and that is when the miracle started. All of a sudden, I heard God speak to me. He said, "Jutta, you need to go to Pocatello and find Michael early tomorrow morning." I hardly remember the rest of the service, and when it ended, I went straight to Dori and Eric's and told them what happened. They said I would be wasting my time since I was just there last weekend. They didn't say it, but their expressions told me they thought I had lost my mind.

Leaving early after breakfast and devotions, I took off to drive to Pocatello again. Getting about thirty miles from there, I received a call from Matt, Michael's neighbor, who I have often called to see if he had seen Michael. He said, "I just saw Michael driving out, and it looks like he is going to work." I don't know if it was the devil trying to distract me, but I just decided to go ahead anyway. I trusted God. When I drove into his driveway and went up to his front door, I saw the screen door was unlocked and so was the house. My heart was beating so hard; I was afraid what I would find. I was praying as I started walking through room by room. His two cats were on his bed, but no Michael. I looked in the closets too because I thought he was hiding and didn't want to be found. There were lots of papers, but I was looking for him—not at the papers. Downstairs where his office and computers were, was a single light. There was no lights on except for that. Finally, I walked through the laundry cellar room and out to the garage. I didn't even notice his car was running and started to look around and there was Michael all covered up and lying on a mat. There was a small speaker with soft music playing. I just stood there, and I thought my heart had stopped. He looked like he was dead. Kneeling down, I realized he had a pulse. My nurse's training jumped into action. I turned off the car and started to shake him. After what seemed like a long time, I finally saw his eyelids flickering. After a while, he mumbled that he had taken something. I thought what? Morphine? I tried sitting him up. He looked like he was going to get sick, so I put him back down and went to get a bucket upstairs. When I returned, I sat him back up, and he started to vomit. I asked him if he wanted me to take him to the hospital and then come and live with me. He said yes that he would and mentioned a letter by the front door. Since my car was just on the other side of the garage door, I opened the garage, and with a bit of his help, got him into the back seat of my car. I closed the garage door and ran upstairs to get the letter he left and went out and drove him to the hospital's emergency entrance where people helped by putting him into a wheelchair. I could finally relax enough to call Dori who was at work teaching. She was shocked.

The doctors said that if I had been any later, he would have been gone between the carbon monoxide and the amount of morphine (100 mg) he took. Vomiting was probably what saved him from a more permanent problem.

Pretty soon, everyone came because I called Jim and Judy and Michael's friend, Louise Lee. They notified the pastor, and soon everyone helped to clear his house since it was in foreclosure, and that was a busy, scary time.

Now I am so blessed to have Michael living with me. From not getting a job, it made him have total social anxiety, so he could not go for interviews anymore. He got some excellent professional counseling here in Hailey, and that was such a gift from God. For his first visit to the counselor, I took him. As Michael told him about his suicide attempt, he said he had planned it for a year, and it was foolproof. He knew he had to do it at that time because he knew I had been there looking for him. He was actually going to do it after Christmas. I said to the counselor that his plan was "not God proof."

Michael now has a job and is well-liked by everyone. I am happy to have him here, and I'm not alone. He helps me, and I really need that on the computer. He can do almost anything because he is very gifted. God is so good to let me enjoy life here in Hailey, and to have Michael here is a special gift from God.

MANFRED, MY HUSBAND, MY FRIEND

Brazil and Argentina Vacation - 2007

Since most of Manfred and his family were born and raised in Argentina, some of the brothers had planned a trip to visit their places of birth and the memories of their years there. His father was a missionary to Argentina. He was single and met there a young woman from Germany, and they were married there. Missionary terms were seven years at the time, so the first five children were born before their first furlough to America on a ship. Manfred was the only sibling born on that furlough in 1935 in Wisconsin. The next four were also born in Argentina. When Manfred was thirteen years old, eight of the family of ten returned to the United States for good, and the two oldest brothers remained in Argentina and became local pastors.

This is just a little background for the reason behind the trip in 2007. There were eleven Berndt's from America and four from Argentina on this journey in the country.

Manfred and I started our trip separately and flew into Rio de Janeiro. We stayed in a nice hotel and slept a few hours after the long trip. Then we walked the beach, and since it was Sunday, it was very packed with people and lots of activities. In the taxi from the airport, we saw so many unfinished houses where people lived and also "shanties." Then arriving at this beautiful hotel made me want to cry. We were lucky we could check in right away at 8 a.m. because we were very tired. The hotel had a great buffet, and we enjoyed a relaxing dinner. After dinner we walked and you could see the famous statue of Christ. I wished we had time to see more, but we were scheduled to fly out to the Iguazu Falls on the Brazilian side the next day. A taxi took us to the falls which were breathtakingly beautiful. It was a fantastic panorama because of the size of the falls. We went to another buffet at that new hotel where we stayed, and that night I was up almost the whole night vomiting. I guess I had food poisoning. By morning I was totally washed out. Manfred slept through it and was ready to go. Carlito, the husband of one of Manfred's brother's daughters, named Miriam, came to our fancy hotel in an old truck to pick us up. At the Brazilian border, we had some trouble because I had thrown out some forms I thought we didn't need any more. Carlito helped us to get through, but we would never be allowed into Brazil again. On the Argentinean side of the border, we saw the three-foot long iguana. It was amazing.

Herbert and his family lived in Comandante Andresito, Misiones. We drove thirty miles on a good highway (Highway twelve) and then turned left on a muddy, red dirt road for about forty more kilometers, down big hills and low valleys, sliding all over in the mud. Our luggage was in the back of the truck covered up. It was a very primitive rough road, and a very scary ride. After two heavy downpours, we finally arrived at Herbert's. It was one of the scariest drives in my life.

Herbert is the third of the ten children, and they live in a nice home by Argentinean standards. After a beer, Manfred was relaxed a bit more; I was still shaking. I had not eaten and only had a Coke that day. This was where we met the rest of the family. We all stayed in a Swiss cabana for the next three days. There were three languages going on all through the dinner at a restaurant and it was, to say the least, very taxing. People spoke Spanish to German and to English depending on who was talking to whom. Very little English was really needed in this area because the local people were German descendants who understood German and spoke Spanish but knew no English. I was called on to help with the language barrier many times because I spoke German. During that time, I had a headache, and all I wanted to do was go back to the cabin to go to sleep. I was worried if I could hold out for three weeks, but after a good night's sleep, I was ready to go again.

The next day we toured the area in Carlito's truck. There were three people in the front seat and six were sitting in folding chairs in the bed of the truck. It was a beautiful sunny day, but I feared for the safety of those sitting in the back and prayed for them. It all seemed to take me back sixty years to my time in East Germany. It seemed like time had stood still in this area of Argentina. We saw tea leaf farms and factories, and the distribution centers for them. Several lumber mills were in the area. They burned old wood waste filling the air with unpleasant smoke. It was a tropical area and the wood would rot during the rainy season, so they burned it.

Mate is a drink of hot tea that everyone passed around and drank a little. This was a custom so common that even in the bus people passed it around. They had a thermos of hot boiling water and kept refilling the tea. I don't know if the whole country did that, but it seemed that way.

An interesting fact on our first day in the area is that many of Manfred's brothers and family wanted to go to the bank to get local money, but only my bank debit card worked. Over our time in the area, I had to take out money for the others. We spent quite a bit of time trying other banks, and everyone of them got pretty frustrated. It was a good thing I had enough money in the bank. It felt weird to take out money for others.

On the first day of the month of November, we all cramped into a ten-seater van and started our tour to see the rest of the country starting with the Iguazu Falls on the Argentinean side. We experienced the falls in a rented raft with supplied rain gear and life vests. It was amazing to see those falls from down there. Actually, it was scary to see the power of the falls all around us. My nephew, who is mentally handicapped, was so scared as the raft went under one of the falls that he was screaming. The float driver thought he was screaming because it was so much fun, so he went under again. I thought Andrew was going to jump out of the raft for fear, so I had to hold him down. His poor heart was pumping like crazy. After we left there, he acted like he was so brave.

Argentina, like all countries that large, has varied landscapes. We visited several small towns where Manfred's dad had started building churches. Most of his father's travel between congregations was by horse and buggy. One of Manfred's nephews, named Marcos, was in charge of an environmental preserve we visited. Also, one of our visits was to a Guarani Indian reservation. It was quite a drive to get in there on an unpaved, hard, red dirt road for nearly thirty miles. It took two-and-a-half hours but was worth it. We spoke with the "Indian Chief." There were thirty-six families living there. They had a school and a clinic. Doctors or nurses visited every two weeks. Almost everyone was barefoot. Most of the people seemed to have bad teeth, and we were told it was because they use sugar cane like we might use gum to chew.

The whole three-week vacation was hard because there was so much to see and do. There were distances to travel, and we ate in many restaurants in the various small towns we visited where there were churches that were started during the twenty-eight years Manfred's family lived there.

The brothers all had different memories from where they spent their youth. It was very touching to hear their stories. At one of the small towns at noon, I walked the whole outskirts of the area and never saw another person. Siesta time is taken very seriously in this area. The dinner hour starts mostly at 8 or 9 p.m., and a lot of meat is ordered. One evening I ordered pork chops and got six of them on a plate and nothing else. You have to order everything else extra. If you order you must be very specific. It was another learning experience. Customs are hard to keep up with in various areas of the country. It sure made me thankful everyday that I lived in beautiful Sun Valley, Idaho, but the local people seemed content.

After visiting the ski area in the southwest which has the snow in our summer, we took an overnight bus to Buenos Aires, the capital of Argentina. I could not sleep on the bus and took a long nap when we got to our hotel. One unforgettable experience was on a crowded subway when Martin, Manfred's brother, who is two years older, was pick-pocketed. He was very angry and then Manfred realized he was also without his wallet. Luckily, he hardly had anything in it but one credit card we quickly canceled. I had the money in a fanny pack that I protected carefully. Buenos Aires is a very busy city, and we enjoyed sightseeing in several different areas within the city. It was interesting to get to know many of Manfred's family better and appreciate them more. But Manfred did not have as many early memories as the others did, especially the siblings who had lived there much longer. It seemed that Manfred was the most athletic one, and his brothers envied him as a boy. He was the only one born in the United States, so he felt a little left out at times.

Thinking back, I believe that on that trip Manfred had his first brain bleed because at times he would not answer questions very well and often seemed agitated when asked, which was not normal for him at all.

In January of the next year, he had another that woke him up in the night, and he said that something was wrong with the clock because it only had two numbers. It was very early on Saturday morning, and he lost his peripheral vision. The on-call eye doctor came and examined him and then Manfred went to the emergency room. The problem was not his eyes but in his brain. It made him feel very insecure which was very hard since he was always so organized and self-sufficient. These were very hard times for both of us because I wasn't sure what was safe for him to still do by himself. After a couple of fender benders, he did not want to drive anymore. That was a big relief; I was afraid he might hurt someone.

This started a whole new chapter in our lives. Manfred had retired from Valley of Peace Lutheran Church in Hailey the year before in 2006. He was still enjoying serving at the church but realized it was time for a change. The church gave him a big retirement party even though we were still going to be coming to church there.

Manfred's Declining Health

One of the most difficult times for me was when I noticed that Manfred seemed to be forgetting things. When Paige was born in 2003, it seemed like he could not remember her name. It was kind of the first hint I can see now looking back. It was also the beginning of slowing down in the church by forgetting what was next.

At our last Berndt family reunion in July 2010 in Estes Park, Colorado, his brothers were shocked when talking to him because of how different he was. One incident was after lunch in the cafeteria, when I told him I was taking my granddaughter Paige to one of the activities there, and that I would be right back. He was sitting with his brothers and family. When I got back, he was standing outside and kept asking everyone where I was. It was scary to me to realize how this confident, hard working, smart man I married and loved for so many years was not the same anymore. We still did a lot of camping together, and he loved to go fishing. He still plowed the snow and mowed the lawn. He still got up early in the morning, and we did devotions and our 10 and 10's.

At church, he was frustrated because he couldn't keep up with the Bible studies and reading. At times during those years, he would get frustrated and say things that hurt, but then always apologized. We still traveled to Arizona and Washington a few times.

He still worked hard and spent a lot of time on the computer and answering people's questions on email. He always talked about wanting to write two books, one about heaven and one on eagles. By 2006, I already had to help him in church when he forgot what was next. The time was right for him to retire. I finally said to him, "If you want to write the book, you need to stop answering questions on email and start committing to write." He did work on it and met with Sue in Pocatello who helped him edit it. Sadly, it never got printed 'til after he went to heaven. *For Heaven's*

Sake is the title of the book. His concern was that people don't really believe in heaven, and he himself, had doubts at first.

In 2003, he had his first stroke that took his peripheral vision. It was scary for him and for me also, but realizing he had small bleeding strokes made me understand it all better and learn to accept the obvious. He was not the same, but I loved him, and God would take care of both of us. I was often amazed how much he could still do and work on the computer to finish his book.

We also went to Victoria, Canada, for his seventy-fifth birthday and celebrated it in a nice bed and breakfast place and went for an English Tea in the Butchart Gardens. It was a wonderful long weekend. After that we went to Margarete's house and celebrated again and also Luke's birthday on the thirtieth of August.

After we got back home at the end of September, we did a Lutheran Marriage Encounter at Camp Perkins. We stayed in our camper there plugged in, and the other three presenting couples stayed in the retreat center. Manfred had experienced many small strokes for three years already, but his body was not affected—just his brain. He was still able to handle everything, but I had changed some of the talks, so it would not be as hard for him. It was very hard for me realizing Manfred needed so much help, but at the end, he preached a great sermon. It was a real "praise God" moment.

It was a great weekend for most of the couples, especially the three couples presenting with us---but also with the eight or ten couples on the weekend. After that weekend, Manfred cleaned all the windows, which was amazing, but he loved clean windows.

On October 5, 2010, Manfred woke up in the morning, and I asked him if he was all right; he said he had a headache. I got up and gave him some Tylenol and got dressed. I got breakfast ready, and he had gotten up and was dressed but did not come to the table. He went and sat on the sofa. In talking to him, I realized he did not answer and just looked at me. It was so weird, but I knew it was serious. I went and got the car out of the garage and parked, so he could get in the passenger seat. Then I took his hands, and he stood up, and I walked him out to the car. He would not bend so that I could get him in, so a neighbor helped me, and I drove him to the hospital. From there they flew him to Boise, Idaho. I drove there and called the children on my cell phone. Margarete could not come at that time. She had four children, and Luke was just five.

He had a massive bleeding stroke which caused him to die ten days later in the hospital in Boise. Richard was holding his hand when he died. I was asleep on a cot in the room and Dorothy and Michael were there, too. Manfred died there on the fifteenth of October. As I write this, my heart rate is racing just thinking about that time. Making the decision with the children by my side to give Manfred no further treatment was one of the hardest things in my life.

This was the end of our Marriage Encounter ministry, but I have the joy of knowing it continued without us until COVID-19 which, I think, ended it. God blessed us with getting to know so many great people around the world. By dialoging daily, we found so much more joy for having each other in this time of retirement and for growing closer to our Lord as well.

Living After Manfred - 2011

After Manfred went to be with Jesus, I knew life was going to be very different and sad, but I also knew that life goes on. Being an organizer, I forgot to really take time to grieve his loss at that time. Planning the funeral with the children there, I was busy right away.

Since the funeral service was going to be in Pocatello, I was thankful for Pastor Dinger and all the members who took care of the planning and serving a big dinner at the church. They did it all. I had hardly anything to worry about. It was clearly a celebration of Manfred's life. I was happy because all my children were present and several of Manfred's siblings and families also were there. We all stayed in the Holiday Inn right by the church, which was such a blessing. Also, Margarete flew in for the second funeral service held here in Hailey by Valley of Peace. That was for the burial service at our cemetery. That was right after we had Thanksgiving here so all the children were present. Manfred had often shared that he wanted a grave stone, so Margarete went with me to decide what kind and what it should say. I'm glad we did that. I know it would have pleased Manfred.

I had a lot of pain in my right hand but put off going to the doctor because of Manfred's health that last year. In February, I finally had carpel tunnel surgery, which was such a big relief. It was probably caused by all the sewing and quilt tying over the years and sewing banners for church.

In March 2011, I went to Germany for what would have been my parents one hundredth birthdays as I have already shared. It was so different for me to go without Manfred at my side.

In June, I celebrated our fiftieth wedding anniversary in Hawaii, which had already been planned quite some time ago. It was wonderful with all our children and grandchildren, but it was also sad for me because Manfred was not there.

Mostly, I started my own day-by-day routine and also went on many special trips like Lake Powell, Scottsdale, and sailing in Panama for one week on a catamaran with Fred and Gale. There were other trips, but it was just not the same without Manfred at my side. We had one more Berndt reunion in Colorado in 2015, and it was great to see so many Berndts and families. I was thankful that Michael was able to come with me and the rest of the family.

Looking back now, because of all the activity around me, I see that I never really allowed myself to grieve for the loss of the love of my life. I think the second year was harder than the first year after his death. I had times of not wanting to get out of bed and often cried myself to sleep. I would discipline myself to get up anyway! I kind of functioned more like a robot. I still did my morning routine of making my bed, having my devotions, and reading the assigned scripture and prayers in the Portals of Prayer, but my heart was not there. I had a hard time to even feel God's love. Everything suddenly felt harder to do. I started walking Bella, Dori and Eric's dog, after they moved to Hailey, and that was like the best medicine for me at that time.

Life went on as the family grew and many of my previous activities became the same as before—visitors, family visits, church activities, travel, and camping. Children going to schools and college, graduations, and just daily routines seemed like the new normal until COVID-19 came along, and many activities had to be canceled. There were hardly any more visitors. Life seemed to slow down and almost stopped. I really missed all those things I had taken for granted for years. I thank God that slowly life seemed to pick up again, but it's not the same.

SOME OF THE FAMILIES AND
PEOPLE SPECIAL TO ME

Looking back on my life by rereading many of the wonderful letters people have written to me on my birthdays, retirement, and even in the volume of Manfred's retirement has helped me see myself closer through the eyes of my friends. Unfortunately, all the friends I've made and still keep in touch with, I know I can't write about them all. Many say very similar compliments about the traits they saw in me that I am now more aware of. There are a few who are especially precious to me, and those are from special friends who chose me to be "godparent" at their baptism. I know God has put them in my life for a reason, and I pray for them often.

One of my godchildren lives in Germany and is a very successful hotel owner. Another one lives in Colorado and was born in Hong Kong. The rest are spread out all over the United States. Aaron, another godchild, lives in Meridian, Idaho, and just got married a year ago and had his first child in April 2021. He is a precious little boy and was given the name, Marshall Manfred Jenkins, the same as my husband's, for his middle name. I felt honored by that and knew Manfred had invested a lot of time in Aaron's childhood by taking him fishing and just spending time with him.

Aaron's parents, Jim and Sue Jenkins, have moved back to Kansas but came to Boise, Idaho, for the baptism. While holding the baby and sitting in Aaron and Melissa's beautiful, comfortable home in Meridian, Idaho, I asked Jim (a grandfather now) how he felt about using Manfred's name instead of his name, Jim, as a middle name. This is what he quoted to me, but not until after a long pause and making me think I had offended him. Then he leaned forward and said, "If it weren't for Manfred, I would be in hell by now." He shared how he saw Christianity as a crutch for insecure and not very bright people. That remark took my breath away, and after a pause, I finally said "What do you mean?" After our visit way back when, he said that after talking with us---especially with Manfred---he couldn't believe how wrong his judgment was. He was crying as he was sharing that with me, as I was also. It was such a shock for me to hear. I had no idea about it. I felt God in the room and was shaking. There were so many years of friendship, and I had no clue. It also made me thank God for it, and it just made me so happy. I just love the Jenkins family. Aaron and his sister, Ruby, both born in Pocatello, are my godchildren. They still come up here to visit me when they come to Idaho from Kansas.

I have a total of ten godchildren. I pray every day for all of them. Many are now adults, in fact all of them, but I still think of them as my children.

I am amazed at what people remember about me. A letter came from Pastor Opsahl and Vi who wrote a letter about Beth, their daughter who was five at the time, and said I was the best role model for her. Beth was thrilled to be our flower girl when we married, and she had kept the dress I made for her all those years ago. Apparently, when Vi called her to share about my sixtieth birthday, she shared that when all the activities from the party were over, she got up on one of the boy's bunk beds in the backroom and looked out the little window and watched Manfred and me drive away. She cried and cried her little heart out and feared she would never see me again. Vi said she never knew about that. She wrote "You were one of the special people in her life." I loved that whole family, especially Beth, the little flower girl.

Another special family is the Nelsons, a young couple who attended Grace Lutheran Church, and she was a teacher at Grace School. When I first met them, they were both single. As I recall, Mark visited Grace Church and lived close to the hospital, so I went to visit him. When I was led into the house, I realized there was no place to sit except the window-sill. There were several guitars and lots of music stuff all around. He sat on a stool and shared about his life. He came from Minnesota. He was attending a small Baptist church but felt his talent was not really used there. He finally attended Manfred's "Basic Bible Truth Class" and became a member and started a contemporary music group for our second morning church service, which was a blessing. He also got to know the young lady who was the teacher and eventually Manfred did their wedding. They had two girls and moved to Portland, Oregon. I was sad to see them leave because the second little girl became my "goddaughter." After a few years they had a son, and when he was still a toddler, they moved back to Pocatello. I was very happy and often carried him around at church. Soon after that we retired and moved away. But they visited frequently, and they loved playing games like me. One of the games they loved was *Uno* because they always won at checkers and other board games.

One year, they came on Palm Sunday weekend, and the three-year-old boy wanted to jump from the bunk bed on top to the big bed, and I wouldn't let him. That made him sad, but I'm glad I did. When they got home the next day, he was not feeling well, and after a couple of days, they took him to the doctor and found out he had cancer. He was diagnosed with a neuroblastoma at the Children's Hospital in Salt Lake City, Utah. It was so sad remembering a little boy I took care of for a year with the same disease when I was a nurse long ago. I understood what the family had to go through and was scared for them and prayed for them every time I thought about it. Because the parents had to spend more time in Salt Lake City, it became harder for the girls. The dad had to get back to work, so Mom stayed with the boy in Salt Lake City. There were times between treatments when he was able to come home. His appetite was not good from the treatments, but he loved Wendy's chicken nuggets. He ended up having to have a bone marrow transplant and during that time, Mom stayed down in Utah. Grandparents from Minnesota came for a while to be with the girls. They both went to Grace School—-the older one in second grade and my goddaughter in half-day kindergarten. I stayed with them for one month to help out. I was amazed at how the girls had adjusted. They got up and got ready for school by themselves and often early, so they had a little time to play. They made their own breakfast and the older one made her own lunch to take. I just helped a bit with brushing their beautiful hair and then drove them to school. I picked up the kindergartener at noon, and we watched the *Brady Bunch* together. We walked, went to the park often, and even visited an older couple from church who lived in the neighborhood. I cooked dinner every night, and the dad would join us after work. We actually had a fun time together.

One evening after prayer time on an evening the dad had gone to Salt Lake City, the older girl broke down crying and banged the wall with her feet. I could feel her anger and just put my arms around her, held her tight, and cried with her, which I'm doing now thinking about it.

The little boy was always in so much pain, and that was so hard on the mom. They decided they needed a break or they would break. They called me and shared how things were going, and said that I was the only person they trusted to be with him while they took a weekend away. Of course, I never thought about it twice and made arrangements to go. It was one of the hardest weekends in my life. He was crying out in pain, so I finally just crawled in bed with him and held him tight. We finally both slept for a couple of hours. I really understood how hard it was for the mom, especially. She looked awful. She was losing weight, and looked just exhausted. I was happy I could, at least, give them a short break.

My last opportunity to help them was holding him on the day before he died at home. The parents went to make funeral arrangements and choose a burial plot. I just sat there holding him in my arms, and every once in a while he would open his eyes and look at me and whisper, "I love you, Oma." He knew he was going home to be with Jesus. I hummed "Jesus loves you, this I know...", and he smiled.

I just feel right now that I am reliving this nightmare. God blessed me so much by putting that family in my life. They now live in Arizona, and I visit them when I go down there. Both girls are doing well, and that makes me happy. I can still see the big bunch of blue balloons and one white one being released after his funeral service at Grace Lutheran.

The Trost Family

Whenever I start thinking of my life here in beautiful Hailey, Idaho, and look out of my living room window, I can't help but thank God. In winter when the mountains are white with snow and the pure blue sky and bright sun shines on the snow---making it look like diamonds glistening everywhere---it puts a song in my heart. I start thinking about all the wonderful people who have added so much joy and happiness to my life at over eighty-five and a half years. Thinking about how people affected my life started way back since childhood, but I'm thinking more about it even more the last few years since my retirement.

One of the couples, the Trosts, have added so much joy and happiness to my life live in Pocatello, and when I go visit my friends at Grace Lutheran Church down there, they always let me stay with them like I belong there. They treat me like family. The letters from them both at my sixtieth birthday and for my retirement make it sound like I did so much for them and their children.

This wonderful friend Judy, the wife, showed me in her letter that since she has known me so long, it was hard to think of one time, so she started rambling. Some of the words she used are "my strength and conviction." Her daughter and son attended the youth group, and she says they both want to model their lives after me. They think I'm the best pastor's wife, supporter, encourager, prayer defender, and faithful lover. She wrote, "You showed our children Christ in you, His unconditional love and the Father's discipline, and the Holy Spirit's forgiveness. You are so special to my children and also to me."

She goes on and on about working with Stephen Ministry, Camp Perkins, and our overnight prayer vigils at the church. Wow! Is that really who I am?

SIXTIETH BIRTHDAY WISHES

To help me move on with my writing, I pulled out our many albums and pictures hoping they would help me realize who I am through the eyes of other people. Many pictures just helped me a little because I could see mostly where we have been in our travels, confirming that we did a lot and saw a lot. They made me feel privileged and blessed, of which I already am so aware.

Finally, I pulled out the big album labeled, "Jutta's Sixtieth Birthday." I can't even express how shocked I was after reading a few of the pages in it. It brought me to tears and many of the letters say similar things, but in some of them they are more specific in the way I was special to them. Each letter made me aware of how much I love the writers of the notes and how much I still love and miss them. After a while, I had to stop reading because my tears were falling down on the plastic covers, and my nose was running. Manfred wrote something too and just the first few pages of his writing made me feel like I couldn't breathe. Even now putting it into writing, I'm shaking. Am I really worthy of that much love and caring? I was not even aware of it, and am I that special only because God made me that way or because of the people He put into my life who nurtured that?

Each of those letters, notes, and cards bring back so many warm feelings, and I wish I could call these people now and thank them for their sharing and love that, I guess, I took for granted.

The first time I glanced through the big volume I was busy with work and planning our big trip. I never really took the time to read it carefully. I'm a slow reader since I never had books when I was young, and I might be dyslexic if those things were even in my vocabulary at the time. No one ever mentioned dyslexia in those early years, and nobody ever talked about this problem in childhood learning until Michael turned six in 1976. Now, I love to read, but my eyes tear from the stress, and I often need to use a magnifying class, especially in my Bible. But reading through all the accolades about what other people shared about who I am is amazing and overwhelming.

Many of the letters or notes point out my strengths, and I clearly see them now, but wasn't really aware of them. Since my job with intravenous therapy, which I started in 1988, took me to almost every area of the hospital, I was, of course, recognized and known. In the short letter from the head nurse on the medical floor, she wrote "You are a bright part of my day, always recognizing every one and having a big smile for each and every one of us here at Pocatello Regional Medical Center. The best thing that you do is to touch me. A small pat on the back or a neck massage gives out this wonderful message that here is someone who truly cares about me and can show that with a caring touch. Not everyone can do that." Another quote from the same letter is, "Some of my most fond remembrances are associated with our special and dear friend, Phyllis. Believe me, Jutta, Phyllis would have been lost without you. It meant a great deal having you stop to visit her each and every day. If you were late dropping by to say, "Hello," she would start to worry about you and wonder "if everything was okay." You helped the family, and it was a relief to them. You were Phyllis' 'special duty nurse.'"

I loved Phyllis, but was never aware that people even knew about my visits with her, except the children and the husband. Seeing me though the eyes of others is heartwarming. My last night with Phyllis, I read from Isaiah 53 to her and Psalm 23, and she shared with her daughter who came to help her get ready for the night, that today I'm ready for the first time to go meet my Lord Jesus, and thank you, God. She died that next morning at 5 a.m. when her husband called me to come quickly because he was afraid to have her die at home.

One of Manfred's great secretaries was also one on my friends. Her husband was a teacher at Grace Lutheran School, too. It was an early time when the church started to use the computers at first, so there was a lot of learning for people who like me, have relied on copy machines. They had two little boys who I loved. They had moved to Washington State after a few years, and I missed them but visited with them while visiting my daughter in Shelton, Washington. For my sixtieth birthday, she sent a letter sharing some of the things that came to her mind as she answered the invitation about the special event. I quote a few that surprised me.

— "Opening your home to us when we moved into town until we could get settled in"

— "Being a babysitter so many times, sometimes for sick kids, sometimes for healthy ones, sometimes for a few hours, once for a week!"

— "Teaching Jacob to tie his shoes"

— "Being Tim's Junior High youth counselor"

— "Being our "Idaho mom/grandmother"

— "Allowing us to use your van for a memorable family vacation to California, and for shorter trips around Idaho, too"

I know this was one of my many special friends, but nothing I did was out of the ordinary as I recall. The times just seemed to blend into my everyday life. I am still blessed by them and even visited them on Victoria Island for a week after Manfred had died. It is so special for me to be able to keep in touch with friends from the past.

Another special couple from the past also wrote a very wonderful letter. This couple was very special at the time of the construction of the new church in Pocatello. They were definitely a huge help to Manfred, as one of the leaders in the church. He always wore a big cowboy hat, as I recall. This is one of the sentences he wrote. "The words of Goethe seem to come to life when put in context with our friend Jutta Berndt: 'The world is so empty if one thinks only of mountains, rivers, and cities; but to know someone here and there who thinks and feels with us, and who, though distant, is close to us in spirit, this makes the earth an inhabited garden.'"

He goes on to write, "You make this world an inhabited garden for so many in every place you meet them, whether at work, church, play, or Marriage Encounter. You and Pastor have been role models for both of us."

This seems so flattering and intellectual, but that is who they are— great people. I just love them and their mother who lived with them. What a joy to just picture them in my mind.

All those people and letters make me look back at how God seems to always take care of me. I just don't feel worthy of it all. It is fun to recall all those times and seeing that God always had a plan for me by the people He put in my life along the way.

––––––––––

In a letter for my sixtieth birthday celebration from dear friends in American Falls, they shared about the times we spent together with Marriage Encounter. I helped the family as a nurse, as well. But to summarize what they wrote in a note to me on my sixtieth birthday was that "…words seem so inadequate for what I had done for them as a family, with the husband's heart attack, with Dad and the son's surgery, and with the nephew's ordeal." The nephew had lost one leg in a boating accident at fourteen or fifteen years of age. It was quite an ordeal since his leg got caught in the motor.

One other thing the mother wrote that makes me laugh was that if I came into her husband's room after his heart attack and he had his legs crossed, I called him on it.

I'm amazed at how many people remember the little things about me that I'm never even aware of.

Some of the letters that I'm re-reading now (if I ever read them before, I don't remember) make me speechless.

When first moving to Pocatello and renewing my license for nursing in Idaho, I worked nights at St. Anthony's Hospital. This is what one of the nurses I worked with wrote for my birthday note, and it shocks me. "I remember back when I first met you and had the privilege of working with you in the old Saint Anthony's Hospital on the night shift in the Intensive

Care Unit. You and I used to take care of a lot of head injuries, and we did a darn good job. You were such an experienced nurse, and you did it with such ease that I was always amazed at all the things you knew and all the ideas you had. I really respected you. I learned a lot from you back then. Another thing that I really admired about you was the way you could talk and stand up to the doctors. You were never afraid to speak your mind, and I especially was tickled with the way you stood up to [a certain doctor] one night, and you caught him speechless. I kept thinking that when I got older, I would be able to get the same respect that you did from your co-workers and physicians, but I have learned that you not only got that from your maturity but mostly from your wisdom and from the "school of hard knocks," and all the experience that you have had, and all the hard work that you have put in."

IN CLOSING - 2/10/2022

Now, every morning when I wake up, the first thought I have is "God, you are so good to me." I open the curtain and the blinds and look out to appreciate another beautiful sunrise and thank God that He allows me to enjoy another day here on earth. I thank him that I feel strong and healthy, and then I prayerfully consider how to spend another day praising him. My joy is knowing that He will guide my every moment and the many people He allows me to pray for during my morning devotions. He supplies all my needs so abundantly that I really have no more anxiety or stress in my life.

Michael, who is living with me now, is a gift from God that I thank Him for daily. So many things I look at in my house bring back memories of the people who have gifted me with them. I never like clutter, but I do enjoy the few things that give me joy like my collection of Hummel figures that are displayed in my bedroom and see every day. They bring memories of my life in Germany and of my family still living there. Some pictures on the walls all have a story behind them, and it makes me thank God for those people and stories.

I thank God for my daughter that lives near me---and all my family---every day, especially for Bella and Sylvia, her dogs. They get all excited when I go and pick them up for our walk in the canyon.

I sold my Roadtrek camper a while ago but still miss it because I enjoyed meeting other campers and getting to know them. So many wonderful, interesting people makes me thankful and helps me become aware of the fact that most people are kind, caring, and lovable—unlike what you see on television. I'm thankful for all the wonderful trips Manfred and I made with the camper over the years. I can still drive, for which I'm grateful, so that I can still go and visit my friends. Most of all, I'm happy to still have friends.

Skype is a real gift from God. I now can see my siblings in Germany and actually know them better than any time in my life since I left home at age fifteen. Yes, I've been blessed to be able to travel to see them, which was wonderful. Now, travel is getting harder, especially with this pandemic, so to be able to Skype is a wonderful option.

Most of all, I thank you, God, now for a life filled with so many people who have guided my life because You placed each one of those people to keep me in the path of the life. I can now look back on a life filled with Your guidance and protection. I know You are with me all the time, and I try to be a blessing to others.

I could go on and on and quote all kinds of Bible passages that I have memorized, but that is not really my style. I love to sing and I sing hymns when I'm alone because of my scratchy voice. I always have a song in my heart!

I thank you, Lord Jesus, that you have allowed me to write these memories down while I still can. Finally, I pray that my life has been a blessing to others.

NOTES

1: The Guidebook Company, Ltd. Hong Kong, China, Guangdong Province. Scale 1:200000. Hong Kong: Pacific Century Publishers, Ltd., 1992.

APPENDIX

Map of Lantau in Hong Kong, China Guangdong Province

Additional Information

(a) Traute and Another Friend from Hong Kong

Sometimes when I'm saying my prayers and standing by the window looking out over the beautiful place God has given me to enjoy, I think of people from my past who have blessed me. Today it is my friend Traute. She is
from Austria, went to the University in London, England, where she met
her husband, Raymond, who was from Hong Kong. After they got married,
they moved to Kowloon, Hong Kong, and got settled.

It was not easy for Traute to get to know people since she did not
speak any Cantonese. I mentioned her before because I met her in a park
after we both had little children and became friends. We often spent time
together to have morning coffee. Her husband's family is large, and she
got to know them quite well, but they were not close to each other. Their
cultures are so different. The two of us had many heart-to-heart talks while
the children were in school.

She grew up in Austria not really attending any church, but considered herself Catholic. Even though my memory seems so long ago, just
thinking about Traute gives me a warm feeling of love for her. Now we still
Skype for birthdays and holidays, and she often shares how God is now
part of her life. All her children are married and have children of their
own and live in Hong Kong. Since her husband died a few years ago, she
has moved into an apartment. She shared with me that hardly any family has a Chinese amah anymore. Now many come from the Philippines.
She says she misses her amah who was the one who helped me during my

depression years ago. Life is really changing in Hong Kong. She is so thankful to God for her children and family.

It's funny—as I was thinking about my lovely Traute, I got a phone call from Hong Kong. The call was from Carol H. I was so surprised but recognized who she was right away. When she was still in high school in the United States, she wrote a letter to Manfred sharing her desire to be a missionary to Hong Kong. She felt called to that place. Manfred recommended she become a deaconess and follow her dream. During our time in Hong Kong, she came and quickly learned the language and adjusted. She went back to the States and married her, then , boyfriend, and they returned. His dream was not the same, so it didn't work out.

A few years later, she returned and has been there ever since and doing a great job working with the women in Hong Kong doing Bible studies. Except for furloughs, she has spent her life serving God there. It was a big surprise to hear from her. She said she was calling donors for general missions with the contacts she had. She saw my name and said it was so much more fun to talk to me since she still remembers the time she spent at our home back then. Most people she calls don't really know her. I had a hard time going to sleep. She called here at 9 p.m. God, you are so good to me.

I do receive her prayer letters twice a year sent out by someone in the States by email. That shows me how much she is doing over there as she shares stories about different women who have learned to love the Lord Jesus.

(b) Hymns That Are Special to Me

The hymn, "Great is Thy Faithfulness," was the song that was chosen for the theme as we started planning the Grace Lutheran Church building many years ago, and it is still one of my favorites. Even recently when we sang it at church, I got goose bumps all over. The reminder of that scary but wonderful time and putting so much prayer into such a big undertaking was a huge faith challenge. Clearly God challenges us every day to live for Him.

The other hymn that often comes to me and sticks with me all day is, "God Be the Glory,

Great Things He Has Done, which is a certain line I can't seem to get out of my mind. When I walk out in the canyon with the dogs each weekday, I think of many Bible verses that I have put to memory over the years, and I hardly notice how quickly the time passes. It's almost like walking with my best friend, Yes, to God be the glory. He continues to hear our prayers."

(c) Youth Group, Cheryl A., and the Dyer Family

When I prayed about starting the Junior High Youth Group at Grace Lutheran Church, which I knew was not really my gift, I had to rely on not only God to help me but also on others to join me in that adventure. "I can do all things through Christ who strengthens me" was one of the verses I hung onto. The biggest blessing was some of the people who were willing to also commit to this, and I got the "cream of the crop" for helpers. By themselves, they decided which part to do according to their gifts. One liked to arrange snacks and another planned activities. Two of us alternated doing the Bible studies. Some just watched for any person who needed extra love and care. It really was a group affair. Without each of the counselors, it would not have been a success.

I had to really step out of my comfort zone doing this. So many wonderful and often needy children didn't allow for the neat and orderly life I was used to. I learned a lot about patience, and trusting other people, and God. It was hard work, but what I recall of that time in my life was a wonderful, rewarding experience. I really got to also know those helpers so much better, and we together, became close friends.

One lady, named Cheryl worked at the university, and we became close. Here are a couple of quotes from her letter to me. "Your humor is delightful and has gotten me through some rough spots more than once. We appreciate your insight and advice given when sought…" Another one was , "Jutta , you are an inspiration to me, in particular, by how you support Manfred in his pastoral work…" She also refers to all the "fun" we had with the youth and lists all the helpers by name, the lock-ins overnight, and how hard it was to keep track of the kids, the food fights, and sledding outings. "Those seventh and eighth-graders were quite a challenge, but, oh, when you know you reached them…what a wonderful, exhilarating feeling!! It was a time of spiritual feasting for me, and I am thankful that you 'twisted my arm' when you asked me to help."

As I re-read this letter, I'm moved to tears seeing how God has blessed that ministry and given me the strength He promised through other people He put into my life. There are so many similar accounts from all those wonderful, caring, and loving individuals.

The Dyers

Because we spent twenty-three years at Grace Lutheran Church, I have many good friends there. Many of these people became members because of Manfred's hard work, but it was also a blessing to me.

I have mentioned this person before when we were at a retreat at Camp Perkins. He had said to me when we heard our house was sold in Pocatello that we should move in with him and his wife, which was very generous. I don't think he ever consulted his wife about it. I guess she was all right with it; she never said. I really didn't know her all that well, but I am so happy now for the time we got to spend with them.

They had one grandson at the time, and I was watching him while the parents worked. They also had two little dogs. When I was not driving to Hailey, I would take walks with the dogs and got to love on the two-year-old, precious boy.

The wife was and still is a good cook, so we got spoiled eating with them at night. Manfred was still working until October. I gave them some money one time, and the man took it and said, "But we don't want any more; we won't accept it." Living with them was very relaxing for me, and fall in Pocatello is so beautiful surrounded by all the mountains and the fall colors. We became more like family than just friends. Even after we moved up to Hailey, every time we went down to Pocatello, we would stay with them. When I was still doing youth group, one of their daughters was part of the group, and she was boy crazy at the time. She was just a real cute, little, petite girl, but I had to always keep a eye on her and sent many prayers up to heaven for her.

One of the best parts of staying at their house was that I saw the girl just recently, and she is a happily married woman, and the little boy there was her son. It just gave me peace to know that God has protected her. My friends also have another daughter who was in college at the time and a younger son who was also in college. I am so thankful how God answered our prayers so many times before we even said them. Gods knows our needs even when we forget to call on Him, and they got taken care of by His care and grace because He loves us so much.

(d) Lutheran Women's Missionary League (LWML)

Of course, I also joined the Lutheran Women's Missionary League. We had monthly meetings locally with Bible studies. We filled mite boxes with coins for mission offerings that went to the National LWML for major church projects. Every two years, we had conventions in one of the churches in the Southern Idaho and Utah Conference. They were fun because the leaders did all the planning, and we enjoyed projects and reports of what was happening in the nation and our District IV. Often on Saturdays, we made quilts for missions—a fun time together serving our God.

A Trip to Canada While Attending a LWML National Convention

I was still active in Pocatello, and in 1993, Manfred joined me to attend the LWML National Convention in Edmonton, Canada. We drove up in our big camper at the time and camped a couple of days on the way up. At the convention, we were surprised by how many people we knew. George and Florence, who were our dear friends in Hong Kong, now lived in Texas and were there. Also, Manfred met a couple of pastors who went to seminary with him and their spouses. There were three women from our church who had flown up for the convention and many others we have known in the past. I love the conventions. They just lift your spirit and make you happy to share time with so many others. There are, of course, business meetings that can seem long at times, but all the worship and singing in such a large group makes you love everybody. They always have great preachers at these events. Then we took the opportunity to see more of Canada. We stayed in the campgrounds where we saw a lot of elk and a black bear as well. We hiked quite a few places. My favorite was around Louise Lake. We had rain one day and slept in, and in the evening, we went to a restaurant to eat just to get out. We also biked many places before heading back to Pocatello.

(e) Stephen Ministry

One of the greatest joys for me was not just serving special people in need or through a difficult circumstance using Christian values, but it was also to get to know a few other people who also work with the Stephen Ministry group so much better that we became friends, not only during the long training to become a Stephen Minister, but also in our weekly sharing of our difficulties and joys of serving.

In every group of people, there are some who have problems that are not well dealt with. It is no different in a church's congregation. Members often come to see the pastor for help, which his great, but he does not have the time to deal with that, and because he understands the issues, he will often suggest that a Stephen Minister might be able to help them over a longer period of time. These problems will vary for everyone. For some it may be depression and for others it may be issues like a death in the family, drug or alcohol use, problems with a child or neighbor, or many times health problems of various kinds.

A Stephen Minister is not trained psychologist and the pastor will tell that to them right away, but they are trained listeners and care givers. Since the pastor knows the problem, he tries to pair people up who would work best for that issue We meet weekly with our care receivers, and once a month we meet together as a Stephen Minister group to be able to share how things are coming along and to see if we might need some help, only we don't ever share who our care receivers are, that is just between them and you.

I learned so much about myself during those times and had to learn that I had to become a much better listener. That took a lot of prayer before each visit to the woman or girl I was assigned to. I was so aware of how important this lay ministry was and how it helped the church, especially the pastor. I know he spent so much time daily trying to serve all the people in his growing and wonderful Grace Lutheran Church.

Over the years I met with a large variety of needing people. I had only four during the several years 'til my retirement. Three of them are now with Jesus in heaven, and one I still pray for and often see when I go to church in Pocatello. She still has some problems but seems to be doing all right. Her husband is very supportive, which is great. Praise God for the people who came up with this ministry and shared it with many other churches.

(f) Valley of Peace

One of the more difficult things here is that we get new people attending, but often they move soon because the standard of living is so very high here. I barely get to know and appreciate them and then they have to, or choose to, move. I was very sad when the Brandons moved, and soon others left after Manfred retired. For worship we had many lay ministers as pastors. It was a very difficult time for all of us at Valley of Peace.

We are blessed now with having another retired pastor here for quite some time. He and his wife have been up here longer than expected, and he is gifted with using the internet.

Since the outbreak of the Corona Virus in 2020, it is wonderful how the internet has helped people who are home bound. Those in church are few, and everyone attending wear masks. It seems to have become the new normal in the world now. Thankfully, a vaccine is now available.

Since Sun Valley is so famous, we do get a lot of visitors, especially in the winter, and it seems the pandemic is far from over. But our little church is hanging in there. Thank you, Lord Jesus!

(g) December 2019 – A Surprise Visit

I went on a surprise visit to see my brother Karl-Heinz (K-H) and his wife, Hannsche, for his eighty-fifth birthday. They had moved from Florida to Manchester, Tennessee, to be closer to family. My nephew Ingo picked me up at the airport in Nashville and took me to his dad and mom's home. They were really excited and could hardly believe their eyes when they saw me. We had a big celebration the next day at Ingo's and Jodi's house. K-H had made his own birthday cake, a schwarzwälder kirschtorte. He used to be a baker in Germany and Switzerland but got allergies to flour and had to give it up. My niece Kirsten from New York and Christina from Florida had come also. It became a big combination birthday and early Christmas party. Kirsten had bought a lot of king crab legs. We ate like kings. I sure had a lot of fun and even did a family hike by the river while I was there. I even suggested we have a special prayer for such a feast and everyone agreed with me, so I got to bless the food and family.

(h) A Visit from Chard and Carrie

My son Richard (Chard for short) and his wife, Carrie, came up to Hailey recently to help me with some yard work. I shared with Chard that I am struggling with this book writing. I told him that I did not want it to sound like a travel log. Then I asked him who would you say I am. I shared that I didn't really know who I am and that makes it hard for me to know how to share.

He started talking about enneagrams. I had no idea what he was trying to tell me. Then Carrie walked in and explained it to me. It's a system of numbers that go with various personalities. She had learned about it and had just received the book she had ordered after she had studied about it and figured out she is a number eight. They both thought I was also a number eight and a nine.

I started reading the book and clearly see why I struggle with writing. After just reading the first part, I realized that I'm a number eight/nine. Number eight is described as an independent, strong, and justice-oriented person. Eights are motivated by autonomy. They have tender, protective hearts toward the weak, marginalized, and hurting. The heading for number eight is Challenger. Number nine is called Peacemaker. They are empathetic and easy-going. Nines are motivated by peace or inner stability and often "go with the flow" to keep peace. Some of the examples talked about just hit me because they describe me and who I am.

This was not just coincidence. It was clear to me that God was helping me since I have been praying about what to do next about writing the book. I felt stuck as to how to proceed. I am aware that what I have written so far is clearly about what my husband and I have done but has not shown who I really am. That makes me think of what Manfred's psychologist said to him. He thought I would not be able to handle retirement because I was too involved with my job. He had been one of my patients a couple of years earlier. At the time I just shrugged it off and was going to prove him wrong. Retirement, at that time, was still a year away.

I am more aware now what I still have to do to show the real me in a lot of the pages I've already written—if that is even possible.

THE END